THE
WINE LOVER'S
—GUIDE TO—
Bordeaux
and Cognac

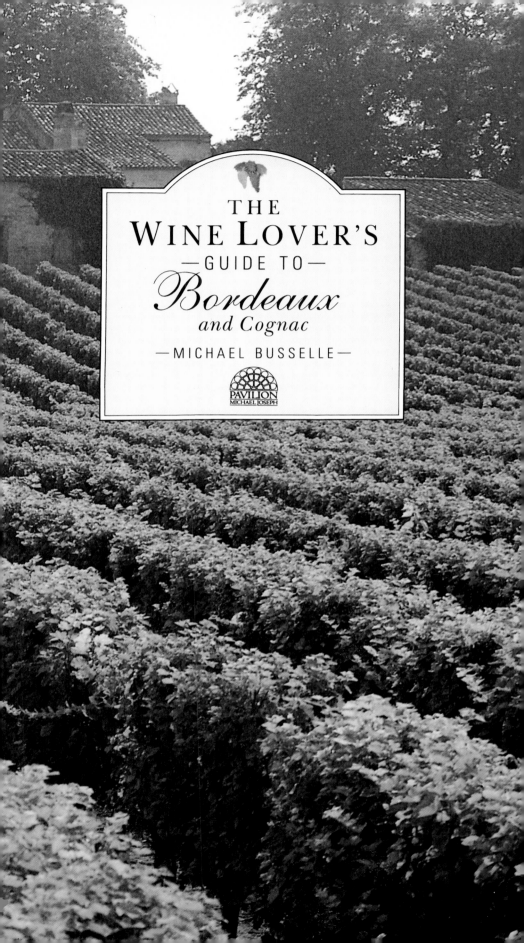

THE
WINE LOVER'S
—GUIDE TO—
Bordeaux
and Cognac

—MICHAEL BUSSELLE—

PAVILION
MICHAEL JOSEPH

First published in 1989 by
PAVILION BOOKS LIMITED
196 Shaftesbury Avenue, London WC2H 8JL
in association with Michael Joseph Limited
27 Wrights Lane, Kensington, London W8 5TZ

Photographs and wine tours text copyright
© Michael Busselle 1986
Wine-buying guides compiled by Graham Chidgey &
Lorne Mackillop © Pavilion Books 1986
Other text by Ned Halley copyright © Pavilion Books 1989

Series Editor Ned Halley
Designed by Bridgewater Design Ltd
Maps by Lorraine Harrison

A CIP catalogue record for this book is available from the
British Library

ISBN 1–85145–248–6

10 9 8 7 6 5 4 3 2 1

Printed and bound in Spain by Cayfosa Industria Grafica

Previous pages: Vineyards near the village of Preignac

Contents

N

COGNAC

COGNAC.
SEGONZAC.
ARCHAIC.
•CHATEAUNEUF–SUR–
CHARENTE
•BARBEZIEUX

N.BORDELAIS

GIRONDE

ST.
CHRISTOLY
–MÉDOC
PAUILLAC.
•BLAYE

THE
MÉDOC
BLANQUEFORT.
•ANDRE–DE–CUBAC
LIBOURNE.
VILLEFRANCHE
BORDEAUX.
•ST.EMILION
BERGERAC
PESSAC.
DODOGNE
LABRÉDE.
MONBAZILLAC.
MONPAZIER

SAUTERNES. LANGON
BERGERAC

S.BORDELAIS
GARONNE

PARIS.

Introduction

The rooftops and church of St Emilion seen from the
road which skirts the southern edge of the town

THE GREAT CITY OF BORDEAUX is the wine capital of the world. Along its quays and boulevards crowd ostentatious buildings from several centuries – brash testaments to merchant wealth harvested over many generations from the famous vineyards that encircle the city. To the west and south lie Graves and Sauternes; to the east, Pomerol and St Emilion. To the north is the most fabled of them all, the Médoc.

Among these fashionable *vignobles* are interspersed the less-renowned but thoroughly worthy *appellation contrôlée* districts that today supply so much excellent 'everyday' claret (red Bordeaux) and fine white wine to wine-lovers no longer able or willing to pay the huge prices demanded for the great *crus classés*. Bourg and Blaye (once more esteemed than the Médoc), Fronsac and the Premières Côtes are examples – as is Bergerac, only a brief journey east from St Emilion.

As a *digestif* to this rich diet of vineyards great and small is Cognac, not far from Bordeaux's northernmost reaches. Here, the vineyards are distinctly back-stage, their crops rendered anonymously down into the most celebrated of all brandies by *maisons* whose fame has spread to every corner of the earth.

The five 'cases for tasting', which are placed at the end of each tour, are intended to provide wine-lovers with a representative selection of the wines and spirits from all these regions. Every one of them is exported, so for enthusiasts who may not be able to safari to the regions in question, an introduction to the fruits of their vineyards should be no farther away than the nearest good wine merchant.

Above: Ripening Cabernet Sauvignon grapes.
Left: A tempting roadside sign to Montagne

Those who do travel in wine districts know, of course, that one of the delights of doing so is to buy the local produce at what might be called the farm gate. But a cautionary note: in the rather grand districts of Bordeaux, the great châteaux are often quite unwilling to sell their wines direct to the public on a retail basis.

Where this is the case, the sensible solution is to make a note of the property's agent in your home country, from whom you are likely to be able to obtain a list of retailers, who probably sell the wine cheaper than you could buy it in France. Very great wines are notoriously more costly in French *maisons du vin* than they are abroad.

Before buying top-rate wine in France from very grand properties such as Lafite and Margaux in Médoc, Ausone and Cheval Blanc in St Emilion or Pétrus in Pomerol, consider the hazards as well as the daunting prices (300FF-plus for good, recent vintages). All the great red wines of Bordeaux are *vins de gardes* – made so they will slowly evolve in bottle to a peak of drinkability that is unlikely to be reached within a decade of the vintage.

Top claret that is ready to drink is virtually unobtainable, except from poorer vintages where less-ripe fruit has made a wine that will mature early into good rather than great condition. So wine-lovers have to buy immature wine from the recent good years before they sell out – and be patient. Vintages generally available now are 1982, 1983, 1985 and 1986 – in,

Above: Compressing the grapes as they are harvested in the vineyards of Fronsac.
Right: The imposing approach to the Château de Malle in the Sauternes region

coincidentally, descending order of greatness. Wines from 1980 and 1984 are available relatively cheaply, for early drinking. These two were comparatively dismal vintages – as was 1987, prices for which are as low as half those for the best years of the decade.

The best value in Bordeaux is unquestionably among the *Crus Bourgeois* – the myriad properties, many of them far grander than the humble appellation suggests, that missed out on the curious 'classification' of estates carried out in 1855. This outdated ranking system, which sets top wines crazily below what are now distinctly homely estates and ignores many of the greatest wines altogether, is misleading indeed to the uninitiated enthusiast.

So don't be deterred by the description *cru bourgeois* on any label. These are the wines to taste and buy *à la propriété* – as humbler estates are happy to offer *vente dégustation*, as well as showing appreciative visitors over their domains. The château is likely to have its own printed tariff for available vintages.

Don't expect any wines from before 1980. The best years to buy now are 1985 and (slightly less good) 1986. If any 1982 or 1983 is on offer at not-too-astronomical a price, snap it up! Do ask questions about the wine: should it be kept a while longer, or drunk soon?

Growers cannot be blamed for hard-selling their wines from lesser vintages such as 1984 and 1987. But don't be lured into buying a case at what seems a bargain price compared to better years. Ask to taste before you commit yourself.

When buying, bear in mind the limitations on duty-free imports. This applies especially to brandy, which is sold direct by *maisons* large and small in the two main centres, Cognac and Jarnac.

Transporting your purchases needs care. Remember that fine wines are a delicate commodity. Left exposed to hot sun in a car, they can easily 'cook' and spoil. Similarly, wines left overnight in the car during the winter could be

A village house in Montagne in the St Emilion region

frozen by a hard frost. This will force the corks out and ruin the precious contents.

The least hazardous way to get acquainted with the wines of these regions is to sample them in the countless *auberges* and restaurants which, in each district, carry impressive *cartes des vins de la région*. The famous communes of the Médoc, Graves and St Emilion have surprisingly few grand restaurants – the Médoc is particularly barren – but the humbler establishments have the special merit of offering local wines at approachable prices.

The cuisine of Périgord influences not only Bergerac, which lies within its southern reaches, but Bordeaux and Cognac too. So *foie gras* (duck or goose liver) and its more affordable imitator *pâté de foie gras* abound. For sheer decadence, eat these with a glass of sweet Monbazillac or Sauternes. The red wines, meanwhile, go down admirably with local specialities such as *magrets* (duck-breast steaks), Pauillac lamb and the vastly diverse game of Périgord.

What tends to impress itself most on the memory during a visit to the vineyards of the region is the architecture. Travel along the famous D 2 through Médoc and you pass extravagant château after extravagant château in a seemingly endless parade of opulence. Enriched by huge and brilliantly successful harvests in recent years, sold at escalating prices to a world market ever thirstier for top wines, the growers are living in a golden age – and spending much of the proceeds on new technology and on restoring their great houses to their former grandeur. Taste the wonderful wines, and you will be hard-pressed to begrudge them a single centime of their success.

The Château de la Rivière between Fronsac and St Aignan

The Northern Bordelais

Above: The Château of Monbadon to the east of Lussac.
Left: The village of Lansac to the north of Bourg

INDISPUTABLY, the wine capital of the world is Bordeaux, an ancient city and river port once the headquarters for Roman troops in Gaul. It lies on the banks of the Gironde and for over 2,000 years has been involved in the wine trade.

To the north of the city are the extensive and highly prized vineyards which start along the northern bank of the Gironde facing the Médoc and reach eastwards beyond Libourne until they give way to the vineyards of Bergerac. This area includes the Côtes de Blaye, Côtes de Bourg, Fronsac, Graves de Vayres, Pomerol, St Emilion and Côtes de Castillon and produces some of the greatest wines of France. The town of Libourne, built on the banks of the Dordogne, more or less in the centre of this region, is second only to Bordeaux in importance as a wine centre. It, too, was an ancient river port, from which the area's wines were exported, and the town has retained its reputation as a wine capital.

THE WINES

All the truly great wines of this region are red. However, white and some rosé wines are made under the general Bordeaux appellation as well as *Côtes de Blaye* (white) and *Graves de Vayres* (red and white), which is just across the River Dordogne opposite Libourne. The main grape types used for the red wines are Cabernet Sauvignon, Cabernet Franc and Merlot, while the Sauvignon Blanc is used predominantly for white wines. Another wine of this region which has its own appellation is *clairet*, a light red wine which is deeper in colour and more full-bodied than a rosé.

Undoubtedly the finest wines of this region are to be found in the small area immediately around Libourne, Pomerol, St Emilion and the surrounding villages of Puisseguin, Montagne, Lussac, St Georges and Parsac, all of which are hyphenated with the name St Emilion, as well as Fronsac, Canon Fronsac and Lalande-de-Pomerol.

THE CUISINE

One of the most typical dishes of this region is *lamproie à la bordelaise*, which is an eel-like, freshwater fish (lamprey) casseroled in a rich, red wine sauce. There is a rich onion soup called *tourin*, which is thickened with egg yolks and cream and served over garlicky bread; often it is enriched with red wine. Among the many types of game found here is *marcassin* (young wild boar); this is delicious when cooked slowly in red wine. The oysters for which the region is famed are often stewed gently in white wine with small sausages called

Above: The church at Fronsac
Left: The imposing façade of the
Château de la Rivière

crépinettes. If you have a sweet tooth you must try the *macarons de St Emilion*, a delicious confection made from ground almonds, egg whites and sweet white wine, which you can buy by the box and make ideal gifts for friends when you get home.

THE ROUTE DES VINS *Michelin maps 71 and 75*

The route given here is not a signposted Route des Vins and not a circuit as such, but it takes you through the most important villages and vineyards and can easily be extended to the regions of Bergerac, Graves or Entre-Deux-Mers. If you are travelling from the north along the Autoroute A10 (*l'Aquitaine*), the best place to start the tour is at Blaye (off the motorway at exit 28 along the D254 and then the N137). The town is situated beside the broad estuary of the Gironde. It is the centre of the Côtes de Blaye, a region not known for any great wines but one that produces a large volume of honest

red wine as well as some white and rosé. Blaye is a charming fortified town surrounded by moats and has an imposing citadel, a fortification built by the famous seventeenth-century military engineer, Sébastien de Vauban; within its walls is a large open park from where you get sweeping views over the river to the island fort, l'Ile Pâte (also built by Vauban), and towards the distant south bank and the vineyards of the Médoc. You can stay at the Hôtel de la

Above: A vigneron with his oak casks
Previous pages: The Château de la Rivière from its vineyards

The brightly painted shutters of a village house near Blaye

Citadelle, which is situated within the ramparts, and there is a Pavillon du Vin in the centre of the town where wines can be sampled and bought.

From Blaye follow the route along the D 669 through Plassac to the village of Thau, where a narrow road, the D 669E, runs close beside the river bank. Here the vineyards sweep right down to the water's edge. Continue on this road towards Bourg. Just outside the town is the Château de Tayac, once the home of the Black Prince; it stands among the vineyards overlooking the river. Bourg, which has its own appellation, is built on the banks of the Dordogne. Its Château de la Citadelle, first built in the thirteenth century and rebuilt in the eighteenth century was once the summer residence of the archbishops of Bordeaux; you can visit the building and wander through its magnificent park planted with magnolias and pistachio trees. The terrace beside the old church commands fine views over the river.

The small village of Lansac is a few kilometres north-east of Bourg; during the Middle Ages, the eleventh-century monastery of La Croix-Davide here was a stopping place for pilgrims travelling to Santiago de Compostella. A little further to the east, near the village of Prignac, are the grottoes of Pair-non-Pair, while just outside the village there is the Cave Co-opérative of Tauriac, where you can taste the local wines.

The wine road continues through the important town of St André-de-Cubzac and then along the D 670 towards Libourne. The vineyards of Fronsac are cultivated in the hillsides to the north of the village and you can follow a narrow signposted wine road through the vineyards and charming small villages such as St Aignan and Saillans. Just to the west of Fronsac is the magnificent Château de la Rivière, dating from the thirteenth century, set

Above: A small château in the vineyards of Montagne near St Emilion
Previous pages: Evening sunlight colours the view of St Emilion

high on the hillside above vast areas of vines; you can visit the château and its *caves* carved into the rock, where the local wine can be tasted.

Libourne, a thirteenth-century *bastide* and once a busy river port, is a bustling town with old quarters and quaysides. This is the trading centre for the wines of Fronsac, St Emilion and Pomerol. The vineyards of Pomerol, which occupy a small area just to the east of Libourne, produce some of the great French wines; you can see the town's tall church spire rising high above the vineyards for miles around. I met an eighty-two-year-old *vigneron* who owned just 1 hectare in the middle of the village. The vines from which he made his wine had been planted by his father, he said, and were over 100 years old.

Among the many important wine châteaux in this area, that of Pétrus is the most highly acclaimed, making a superb wine from the Merlot grape. You could easily pass by without noticing it since, like many of the other châteaux here, it is a relatively modest and low-key building, quite unlike the magnificent, ostentatious examples found in the Médoc. Just across the river from Libourne are the vineyards of Graves de Vayres, and there are two châteaux in this region which are worth visiting too: Château de Vayres, with a riverside park, and Château le Grand Puch, surrounded by ancient farm buildings and vineyards.

The Route des Vins now leads up to St Emilion, an ancient wine village where the Roman poet Ausonius is supposed to have lived. Its narrow, winding cobbled streets are lined with lovely pale medieval houses built of the

The 14th-century Château des Tours near the village of Montagne

local limestone, with rust-coloured slate roofs. There are ruins of Dominican and Franciscan convents, and the fourteenth-century cloisters of the Collegiate church are superbly proportioned. St Emilion has a wine museum and many ancient tasting cellars, together with shops and hospitable restaurants. You could stay in the Hostellerie de Plaisance, a hotel sited on a terrace overlooking the village.

From here numerous quiet roads lead through the vineyards to small villages such as Montagne, which has a handsome Romanesque church, Lussac, Puisseguin, where there is a Maison du Vin, and Parsac, all of which have their own appellations. There are three châteaux you can visit on the way. The first, Château des Tours, is near Montagne; it dates from the fourteenth century, has a Renaissance façade and is set in an elegant park surrounded by vast areas of vineyards. The next is near the village of St Georges. Finally, a kilometre or so to the east of Puisseguin, high up on a wooded hillside, is the fourteenth-century feudal château of Monbadon looking down over the vineyards that carpet the valley below. From here the route continues through the vineyards to the villages of St Gênes-de-Castillon and Belvès to Castillon-la-Bataille, an historic town which is the centre of the Côtes de Castillon and is the eastern limit of the vineyards of the northern Libournais. The vines continue, however, almost without a break to the start of the Bergerac Route des Vins. Alternatively, you can head south towards Sauveterre-de-Guyenne, exploring the villages and vineyards of Entre-Deux-Mers on the way.

A Case for Tasting

THE REGION EMBRACES two of the great Bordeaux wine districts, St Emilion and Pomerol. The softly fruity reds, made largely from Merlot grapes, are ripe for drinking at a younger age than their famous Médoc counterparts. The same goes for the region's humbler wines, from good-value districts such as Fronsac, Bourg and Blaye.

CHATEAU PLINCE
POMEROL
1978

APPELLATION POMEROL CONTROLÉE

HPA 043 - Alc
MOREAU
PROPRIÉTAIRE A POMEROL (GIRONDE) FRANCE
MISE EN BOUTEILLES AU CHATEAU 75 cl

GRAND VIN DE BORDEAUX

CHATEAU L'ESCADRE
1ères COTES DE BLAYE
APPELLATION 1ères COTES DE BLAYE CONTROLÉE
1982
GEORGES CARREAU & FILS
PROPRIÉTAIRES A CARS - GIRONDE
MIS EN BOUTEILLE AU CHATEAU
PRODUIT DE FRANCE 75cl

CHATEAU
FOMBRAUGE
SAINT-ÉMILION GRAND CRU
APPELLATION SAINT-ÉMILION GRAND CRU CONTROLÉE
1985
Sté DE FOMBRAUGE A St CHRISTOPHE DES BARDES - GIRONDE - FRANCE
MISE EN BOUTEILLES AU CHATEAU
ALC. 12,5 % Vol. PRODUCE OF FRANCE 75 cl

CHÂTEAU PLINCE

This small estate makes powerful full-bodied Pomerol, unusually rich compared to neighbouring wines of similar price. Although inexpensive, it is a red wine to keep for five to ten years before drinking, especially from good vintages such as 1982 and 1985. 60FF.

CHÂTEAU L'ESCADRE

From the Premières Côtes de Blaye, northern neighbour of Bourg, on the opposite bank of the Gironde river from the Médoc, come some very good-value clarets. L'Escadre, soft and juicy and for drinking young, is a particularly likeable one. 30FF.

CHÂTEAU FOMBRAUGE

Danish-owned, this big estate belongs to the third rank of St Emilion, the *Grands Crus*. The wine is typically soft and supple, with an intensity of fruity flavour that belies its relatively modest price. Best at five or more years old. 60FF.

Vieux Château Certan
Grand Vin
POMEROL
1983

Appellation Pomerol contrôlée
SOCIÉTÉ CIVILE DU VIEUX CHATEAU CERTAN
Héritiers de Mr et Mme Georges THIENPONT e 75 cl
PROPRIÉTAIRE A POMEROL - FRANCE
MIS EN BOUTEILLE AU CHATEAU

1970
CLOS L'ÉGLISE
GRAND CRU
POMEROL
APPELLATION POMEROL CONTROLÉE
MOREAU, PROPRIÉTAIRE A POMEROL (GIRONDE)
MISE EN BOUTEILLES AU CHATEAU

SAINT-ÉMILION 1er GRAND CRU CLASSÉ

Château Pavie
Appellation St-Emilion 1er Grand Cru Classé Contrôlée
1982
VALETTE
PROPRIÉTAIRES A St ÉMILION (GIRONDE)
75 cl PRODUCE OF FRANCE

VIEUX CHÂTEAU CERTAN

One of the greatest wines of the Pomerol district. The 19th-century château is quite beautiful, and ideally situated amid its 30 acres of vineyard on the best part of the Pomerol plateau. Light by Pomerol standards, but lush and smooth in good years such as 1983 and 1985. Drink from ten years old. 220FF.

CLOS L'EGLISE

The property takes its name from its proximity to the ancient site of a church of the Knights Templar at Pomerol's centre. The wine is well made in small quantities – only about 2,000 cases a year – and is good value for such an elegant example of this expensive district's better produce. 120FF.

CHÂTEAU PAVIE

Largest of the dozen *Premier Grand Cru Classé* estates that are ranked the best of St Emilion, Pavie is a comparatively inexpensive wine among its costly peers. But its quality is unquestionable: rich, ripe and concentrated in recent great vintages such as 1982 and 1983 – for drinking not before the late 1990s. 200FF.

CHÂTEAU DE LA RIVIÈRE

Fronsac might be less fashionable than St Emilion and Pomerol, but it is quite capable of producing wines of competitive quality. The sublime red wine of la Rivière, made at the spectacular château overlooking the Dordogne river, is an ideal example. Drink the lovely 1985 from the early 1990s. 100FF.

CHÂTEAU SOUTARD

Although Soutard is just one among 70 *Grand Cru Classé* estates – the second rank of St Emilion – it produces consistently wonderful wines that seriously rival those of the top châteaux. Fine dark colour and lovely vanilla bouquet. Keep good vintages such as 1982, 1983 and 1985 for at least 15 years. 100FF.

CHÂTEAU DE LA GRAVE

This charming château of the Côtes de Bourg produces a good example of the fruity, easy-to-drink red wines typical of a relatively unknown, but nonetheless admirable, district. Good value wine for drinking within five years of the vintage. 30FF.

CHÂTEAU BARRAIL-BEAUSÉJOUR

If Bourg and Blaye are obscure then Castillon – home of this property – is almost unheard of. That is a pity, for this district west of St Emilion makes some excellent, fully-fruity reds, such as Barrail-Beauséjour. Much cheaper, and often better, than minor St Emilions. 20FF.

CHÂTEAU LAMOTHE

The appellation Premières Côtes de Bordeaux applies to quality wines made along a 40-mile strip east of the Garonne river. Good dry whites and *clairet* (pink) wines, and some fine reds such as the outstanding Lamothe, rich and full-bodied, for drinking after five years or so. 30FF.

ENTRE-DEUX-MERS

This large appellation takes its 'between-two-seas' name from its location between the diverging tributaries of the river Gironde. It produces a veritable ocean of fresh, dry white wine, mainly from the Sauvignon grape. At its best within a year or so of the vintage. 20–30FF.

The Médoc

Above: The grand entrance to Château Beychevelle near St Julien
Left: Young vines surrounding Château Latour in the Commune of Pauillac

*I*N THE FAMOUS CHÂTEAUX and vineyards of the Médoc you experience all the mysteries of the great wines – the aristocratic shades of colour, the myriad fragrances, all the subtleties and sensations of tastes, the fine distinctions between vintages. The Médoc is situated on a peninsula about 100 kilometres long, extending from just north of the city of Bordeaux to the Pointe de Grave, immediately opposite the seaside resort of Royan. It is bordered by the wide estuary of the Gironde to the north and by the vast pine forest of the Landes to the south.

The vineyards run for almost the entire length of the peninsula on a low-lying, gravelly hill range, in a band about 10 to 15 kilometres wide. It is divided into two areas: the Médoc to the north, as far down as St Seurin-de-Cadourne, where the lesser wines are produced, and the Haut-Médoc, stretching from St Seurin to Blanquefort. It is in the Haut-Médoc that the finest wines and the most famous place-names are to be found – St Estèphe, Pauillac, St Julien and Margaux.

THE WINES

The wines produced here are predominantly red. The finest are made mainly from the Cabernet Sauvignon and Merlot grape types, but the Cabernet Franc, Petit Verdot and Malbec are also grown. The classification method of the Médoc wines originated in 1855, when the *Cru Classé* system was

The gateway of Vauban's Fort Médoc close to the banks of the Gironde near Cussac

instigated by Napoleon III for the Exposition Universelle de Paris; the system is essentially the same today. The Classification ranges from *Premier* to *Cinquième Grand Cru Classé* through *Cru Bourgeois* to the basic *appellation contrôlée* Médoc. The way the vines are grown and the wine produced is strictly controlled, even to the method of pruning, and the best wines must come from vines that are at least ten years old. Many vines remain productive for up to eighty years, by which time they will have driven their roots down through the meagre soil to a depth of 3 metres or more. Although the quality of the wine improves as the vine ages, fewer grapes are produced, a factor which contributes to the dramatic difference in cost between a fine wine and a good one. As in all the best wine-producing regions, both the climate and the soil are such that the vine has to struggle to survive; ironically, it is usually these very conditions which create the best and most subtle wines.

THE CUISINE

The speciality of Bordeaux is dishes served *à la bordelaise* – in a sauce of red wine and meat stock with tomatoes, shallots, herbs and seasoning. *Cèpes à la bordelaise*, large, brownish wild funghi with a firm meaty texture, are often served in this sauce. Lamb from the low-lying meadows around Pauillac on the Gironde Estuary is highly prized and saltwater fish and shellfish feature strongly on the local menus too. *Gravettes*, oysters found only in the Arcachon Basin a little to the south of the Médoc, and greatly sought after, have a unique, delicate flavour reminiscent of hazelnuts.

An old house overlooking the Gironde in the riverside town of Pauillac

Above: The monolithic bottle which towers over the vineyards of St Julien
Right: Château Palmer, in the small village of Issan

THE ROUTE DES VINS *Michelin map 71*

The Route des Vins in the Médoc is a single road which runs through the narrowish region, with smaller roads leading off to individual châteaux – indeed it is really much more a tour of the châteaux. A château in wine country can mean almost anything from a magnificent building to a modest farmhouse or even a bungalow; here they tend, very much, towards the magnificent.

There is an element of formality to observe when visiting some of these châteaux: many prefer visitors to make appointments. These can be made through the various *Maisons du Vin* in the region. There is one in Bordeaux, near the Grand Théâtre, and others in Pauillac, St Estèphe and Margaux; they provide a wealth of other useful travel information.

The signs indicating Circuit du Médoc refer to three general tourist circuits which will take you to the beaches, lagoons and forests as well as to the vineyards; if you have the time and the inclination this can be an ideal way of exploring the region. But the route suggested here concentrates on the villages, vineyards and châteaux associated with wine.

The tour starts at Bordeaux. Leave the ring road around the city at Exit 7 and head for Blanquefort on a road which runs through the heart of the vineyards. Near here is Taillan, the first of the many impressive châteaux you encounter in the Médoc. It dates from the early eighteenth century, is set in lovely grounds and has an ancient double-vaulted *cave*; as well as making wine, the proprietor raises thoroughbred horses. The Château de la Dame Blanche where, according to legend, the ghost of a beautiful Moorish

One of the numerous fishing platforms projecting from the reedy banks of the Gironde

princess, Blanca, can be seen riding her winged horse around the castle, is here too: both the château and the town of Blanquefort are named after her.

From this point the route continues along the D 2 to Cantenac. The prestigious wine châteaux are concentrated around this very flat region where there is only a slight suggestion of rise and fall in the landscape: the highest hills you can see are on the other side of the wide, muddy Gironde river in the Côtes de Blaye. Woods and meadows dominate the landscape at this point. You can visit Château Prieuré-Lichine, the domain of the famous wine writer Alexis Lichine; he has a collection of fire-backs from all over the world decorating the courtyard.

Just beyond Cantenac is Issan. There are two châteaux in this tiny village: the seventeenth-century moated Château d'Issan in a peaceful wooded setting along a small lane to the east of the village, and the immaculate Château Palmer, turreted and impressive, set beside the main road. The next village is Margaux: its château is one of the most famous in France – and deservedly so. Its Empire-style façade is framed by an avenue of plane trees. Although the château is a private home, its *chais* can be visited: the wine made here is one of the *Premiers Crus* of the Médoc.

The route continues northwards through a succession of small villages: Soussans, then a detour to Moulis, which has a delightful twelfth-century Romanesque church, and Listrac, then back to Arcins, and Lamarque. Few of the villages are noteworthy – they often consist of a few rows of rather austere, single-storey terraced cottages – but they are invariably brightened up by a blaze of flowers. As an antidote to the low elevation of the houses and some châteaux, the church steeples are remarkably high. The church in Lamarque, for instance, has two enormous towers; there is an imposing château-fort here too, built in the eleventh century to resist the Viking invasion. A short distance further along the route a sign indicates a small road to the east leading to Fort Médoc, in a quiet place close to the river. It was built by Vauban during the reign of Louis XIV as part of a three-pronged defence line (with l'Isle Pâte and the Blaye citadel).

A few kilometres further on, you reach the vineyards of Château Beychevelle, looking down over the river. The name of this grand château is said to be derived from the command to passing ships to '*Baissez les voiles*' (lower the sails) in salute to the Duc d'Epernon, an admiral who lived here in the seventeenth century; the château's emblem is a ship with lowered sails. A small road beside the château goes down the river-bank, an ideal place to sit and watch the boats go by, or to watch the fishermen work their huge nets which they suspend from a gib at the end of a little pier. Many of the beautiful Médoc châteaux can be seen from the wine route. Often they are clearly signposted and you reach them along quiet lanes deep in the countryside; none is more than a few kilometres either side of the D 2.

You can't miss the village of St Julien. It has a large notice somewhat immodestly commanding passers-by to salute its celebrated vineyards; the point is reinforced by a gargantuan wine bottle beside the road. Just to the

Château Pichon-Longueville-Baron, a neighbour of Château Latour

north are two châteaux which you should not miss: Pichon-Longueville-Baron, an elaborate, multi-turreted building, and along a small road to the west, Latour, one of the *Premiers Crus* of the Médoc.

Next you come to Pauillac, situated beside the now very broad river. It is the largest centre on the Route des Vins and has the atmosphere of a seaside town (which it very nearly is), with its wide tree-lined promenade, a busy harbour, pavement cafés and relaxed atmosphere. In addition to Château Latour, two other *Premiers Crus* lie within the commune of Pauillac: Château Lafite-Rothschild and Château Mouton-Rothschild. They are quite close together to the west of the D 2 north of Pauillac. You can hardly miss the ostentatious Château Cos-d'Estournel, which is right beside the road and has

Above: The façade of Château Cos-
d'Estournel in St Estèphe
Left: Château Pichon-Longueville-Baron
in the commune of Pauillac
Previous pages: Château Margaux, built
in the early 19th century and home
of one of the world's greatest wines

ornate, oriental-style turrets and façade. This domain is within the most
northerly of the great Haut-Médoc communes, St Estèphe.

The wine route continues beyond St Estèphe, at times running alongside
the river, to the small villages of St Seurin-de-Cadourne and St Yzans-de-
Médoc, where the Château Loudenne dominates the hills to the west of the
road. The small village of St Christoly-Médoc marks the northern limit of the
wine route. Although there are some vineyards further north these are mainly
for the production of the more anonymous, basic Médoc wines. From here
you can return towards Bordeaux by taking the D 103 E5 to Lesparre-Médoc
and then the fast main road, the N 215, straight back through St Laurent-et-
Benon and Castelnau-de-Médoc.

A Case for Tasting

THE MÉDOC IS HOME TO many of the best red wines of Bordeaux – and of the world. Among them are 61 *Grand Cru Classé* estates (variously ranked from first to fifth quality), crowded alongside scores of humbler – but not always inferior – *Crus Bourgeois* into famous appellations such as Margaux, Pauillac, St Julien and the Haut-Médoc.

CHÂTEAU LYNCH-BAGES

A *Cinquième Cru Classé* in the Médoc pecking order, Lynch Bages is known by the *cognoscenti* to be a much greater wine that its lowly ranking suggests. Like Lafite, the estate is in the Pauillac commune (district), and the wine is tremendously rich, generously fruity and long-lived. The 1982 (to drink from 1995) is superb. 200FF.

CHÂTEAU POTENSAC

A *Cru Bourgeois* from the humble-sounding Médoc appellation, this property is a high-flyer. Owned and run by Michel Delon, who is winemaker at the revered Léoville-Las-Cases, Potensac has great depths of rich, almost spicy, flavour. It needs, in good years such as 1982, 1983 and 1985, ten years' or more of bottle ageing. 90FF.

CHÂTEAU D'ANGLUDET

Although it has no *cru classé* status, this property in the Margaux commune has lately been making wine to compare with many a *Quatrième* or *Cinquième cru*. D'Angludet has the sweet and enticing nose for which Margaux wines are noted. Best vintage ever is the 1983 – to drink from the early 1990s. 100FF.

CLOS DU MARQUIS

This is the 'second' wine of a top St Julien property, Château Léoville-Las-Cases. Clos du Marquis is made from the grapes of younger vines on the estate, and is thus a less concentrated – but nevertheless recognizably ripe and finely scented – version of the *grand vin* of Las-Cases, at half the price. 100FF.

CHÂTEAU LAFITE

Ranked '*Premier des Premiers*' in the celebrated classification of Médoc wines in 1855, Lafite is – on paper at least – the greatest red wine of the region. Owned by the Rothschilds since 1868, Lafite is now run by the charismatic Baron Eric. The wine is an appropriately aristocratic *vin de garde* not to be drunk – in the case of great years such as 1982 and 1985 – before the next century. 400–500FF.

CHÂTEAU CISSAC

Beloved of dedicated Bordeaux enthusiasts, this *Cru Bourgeois* estate of the Haut-Médoc appellation makes a true *vin de garde* – dark, tannic wine, rich in lush fruit, which needs a good ten years' bottle ageing in good vintages such as 1982, 1983 and 1985. Classic claret at a relatively modest price. 80FF.

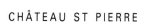

CHÂTEAU ST PIERRE

Smallest of the 11 *crus classés* that crowd the compact St Julien commune, St Pierre produces full, soft red wines that make ripe and delicious drinking about ten years after the vintage. The 1981 (the last to be labelled with the former name, St Pierre-Sevaistre) is outstanding, and the 1982, 1983 and 1985 are also very good. 140FF.

CHÂTEAU MEYNEY

Owned by the respected firm of Cordier (whose other Médoc properties are Gruaud Larose and Talbot, both *crus classés* in St Julien), Meyney is a *Cru Bourgeois* of the St Estèphe commune. The district's wines have a reputation for rich heftiness and long life, and Meyney is an excellent, good-value example. 70FF.

CHÂTEAU LA CARDONNE

Bought in 1973 by the Rothschilds of Lafite fame, this Médoc *Cru Bourgeois* is showing the benefits of the lavish investment made in replanting the vineyards and improving the winemaking technology. A juicy 'everyday' claret. Sadly, the only thing about it that even remotely resembles Lafite is the label! 50FF.

CHÂTEAU FOURCAS-DUPRÉ

One of the handful of *Bourgeois* properties in the Listrac commune, where high proportions of Merlot grapes are commonly used to make soft, easy clarets for drinking quite young. Fourcas-Dupré produces consistently rich and robust wines. At their best when five or six years old. 50FF.

CHÂTEAU CHASSE-SPLEEN

Allegedly, the curious name of this *Cru Bourgeois* estate in the Moulis commune derives from Lord Byron's remark that an infusion of its wine would 'chase away spleen' – in other words, soothe anger. A glass of the rich, darkly elegant red wine from recent great Chasse-Spleen vintages such as 1982 and 1983 proves the poet's point! 100FF.

CHÂTEAU BEAUMONT

This *Bourgeois* estate of the Haut-Médoc uses a large quantity of Merlot grapes in its wine, producing soft and early maturing claret that makes easy, enjoyable drinking within five years or so of the vintage. A likeable introduction to red Bordeaux, at reasonable prices. 50FF.

The Southern Bordelais

Above: The Semillon grapes, used for making Sauternes
Left: Early summer in the vineyards around Preignac

HE NAME GRAVES means gravel – and gravel is what the vines of Graves grow on, over a bed of clay. In fact, this type of soil is characteristic of most of the region, but it is only the wines of Graves that take their appellation directly from the earth in which they thrive. In many ways Graves is an extension of the Médoc, but whereas the Médoc is influenced by the geological formations of the broad estuary of the Gironde river, the vineyards of Graves are cultivated on the terraces of the river Garonne.

THE WINES

The wines of Graves are both red and white. The whites are made from the Semillon, Sauvignon Blanc and Muscadelle grape types and the reds from the Merlot, Cabernet Franc and Cabernet Sauvignon, with a proportion of Malbec and Petit Verdot. As well as dry white wines, France's best sweet dessert wines – *Sauternes* and *Barsac* – are made in this region. These wines are made from Semillon, Sauvignon and Muscadelle grapes which have developed *pourriture noble*, or 'noble rot'. This is a fungus called *Botrytis cinerea* which grows on the grapes, encouraged by the micro-climate peculiar to the region – high daytime summer temperatures combined with damp, misty mornings and evenings. Botrytis makes the grapes over-ripe; their sugar content increases, while the volume of juice decreases and becomes very concentrated. When the juice is fermented it produces a sweet wine which attains a level of alcohol of between 14 and 15 per cent. Because all the grapes do not reach the optimum degree of over-ripeness at the same time, the

Above: Vineyards near Bommes
Right: Making music at a
wine festival in the village of
St Selve in the Graves region

harvesting has to be carried out over a period of many weeks – when the grapes have reached this critical stage – thus the same vine may be gleaned many times, virtually a bunch at a time, and this makes the best of these wines very expensive.

THE CUISINE

The cuisine of Graves is, not surprisingly, similar to that of the Médoc and other regions of the Bordelais. A delicacy which you will find in most restaurants in the region is the large freshwater fish *alose* (shad). It has a firm white flesh with an almost buttery texture, and its flavour is quite distinctive. You will also see *esturgeon* (sturgeon), a fish which is caught in the Gironde Estuary and is often served *à la bordelaise*. *Daube bordelaise* is beef cooked with wine, onions, garlic and bacon rind, then sliced thinly; the reduced sauce is

then poured over it and chilled to form a jelly. Another popular dish is *oignons à la bordelaise*, large onions stuffed with chopped chicken-livers and truffles then baked in a white sauce. Steaks grilled over the glowing embers of vine prunings are very much a speciality of this region; the aroma of the wood imparts a wonderful flavour to the meat.

THE ROUTE DES VINS *Michelin maps 71, 75, 78, 79*

The ring-road around Bordeaux makes a good starting place for this Route des Vins (which is partly signposted).

Bordeaux is a sprawling city which, over the years, has encroached on some of the traditional vineyard areas; indeed many of them are now within its outer suburbs, including one of the most prestigious claret-makers, Château Haut-Brion. It is in Pessac, which can be reached by leaving the ring-road at

The 17th-century Château de Malle in the commune of Preignac

exit 14 and driving for a short distance towards the city centre. Samuel Pepys recorded the wonderful qualities of this superb French wine 'Ho Bryan' in his diary. In 1855, when the official classifications were established, Haut-Brion was the only wine outside the Médoc to be accorded a *Premier Grand Cru Classé*. Close by, and originally part of the same estate, is the Château la Mission-Haut-Brion, where the dates of the best vintages of the last century are inscribed in gold on the roof of the adjoining chapel. Also in the vicinity are Château La Tour-Haut-Brion and Château Laville-Haut-Brion. Drive a few kilometres to the south of Bordeaux, on the D 111, to the village of Cadaujac, the site of Château Bouscaut and Château Carbonnieux. The latter, known for its white wine, was owned by the Benedictine monks of the Abbey of Ste Croix-du-Mont who, it is claimed, exported their wine to Turkey as 'mineral water of Carbonnieux' in order to satisfy that country's religious laws and its sultan, who was very fond of their product.

A number of important vineyards and châteaux are found close to the town of Léognan. A sign on the D 111 indicates the Route des Graves, which guides you around the region. Of particular note are Château Haut-Bailly and Château La Tour-Martillac. In this part of the Graves the vines are not cultivated intensively and there are large areas of woods, pine forests and meadows. A short drive from Léognan will bring you to the village of Labrède where you can visit Château de la Brède, the family home of the eighteenth-century political satirist Montesquieu; it is just outside the village in a wooded setting and is open only at weekends and holidays. The small village of St Selve, a few kilometres away, holds a lively, colourful wine fair in the streets and the church square on the first weekend of June.

Continue south on the N 113 for a short distance to the Sauternais, where the sweet dessert wine is produced. The wine has been famous since the twelfth century, and Richard Lionheart is said to have had a weakness for it. The Sauternais has its own wine circuit which is clearly signposted from the N 113 just south of Barsac or from the village of Preignac, a little further south. These are two of the five communes of the region, the others being Fargues, Sauternes and Bommes. The route winds its way through a series of quiet country lanes to each of these small villages in turn. The countryside here is captivating with its meadows and farmland, its vineyards, and the gently rolling hills with woods and pine forests. Preignac and Barsac are both busy villages situated beside the main road, and close to Preignac is the elegant Château de Malle, set in beautiful formal gardens, where visitors are welcome.

Sauternes is a small, sleepy village nestling in a hollow, surrounded by vine-clad hills. At the Maison du Vin in the square you can use the information service as well as taste and buy wines. The many châteaux in this region are clearly signposted along the way, with the rather extraordinary

*Château de Roquetaillade, which dates from the 12th century,
is just to the south west of Sauternes*

exception of the famous Château d'Yquem. This is because, I was told, 'There would be too many visitors'. You will be welcome though, if you do take the trouble to find it – not too difficult, since it occupies a prominent position on a hill-top near Sauternes. The lovely château is built on the site of a fortress and dates back to the twelfth century although it was heavily restored in both the sixteenth and eighteenth centuries. Thomas Jefferson visited it in 1787, and today it is the venue for the Bordeaux May Music Festival. The estate has over 160 hectares of vines, of which 120 are entitled to the appellation. Every year 2 or 3 hectares are uprooted and replanted and it is then a further six years before they are productive. The equipment used in the château's wine cellars is surprisingly modest – just three presses, a crusher and a wooden *émietteur*, enough to handle only about 4 hectares of normal vines. But because of the unique way in which Sauternes is made, the cellar needs only to deal with one day's selective harvesting at a time.

*Above: A contented villager in the
village of St Croix du Mont
Left: Château d'Yquem a name
synonymous with the sweet white
wines of Sauternes*

Although not on the Route des Vins circuit, the fortified Château de Roquetaillade, which dates back to the twelfth century, is worth a short detour; it is set on a hill in a park and looks just the way a medieval castle should, with battlements and towers.

The limit of the Graves region is just south of Langon (*Michelin Map 79*), a busy market town situated beside the Garonne. Here there is a Maison du Vin de Graves (there is also one at Podensac) and the well-known hotel–restaurant of Claude Darroze, making it an ideal base from which to explore the area. You can cross the river to the long-established wine town of St Macaire, also known for its sweet white dessert wines. Head back northwards on the D10, which stays quite close to the river and passes through a succession of interesting and charming wine villages. A kilometre or so to the east, high up on the hill that borders the Garonne, are the delightful villages of Verdelais and Ste Croix du Mont – Henri de Toulouse-Lautrec is buried in the church at Verdelais, standing at the end of a lovely promenade shaded by plane trees. Ste Croix du Mont has the appellation *Grand Vin Liquoreux de Bordeaux*. Right on the edge of this village, on the hill beside the church, is a terrace with wonderful views over the Garonne Valley and the Sauternais – there is a Maison du Vin in the château nearby. This is particularly appealing countryside, threaded with tiny lanes on rounded hills.

A little further north, the small village of Loupiac also has its own appellation for dessert wines, as does its neighbour Cadillac and the village of Cérons, across the river. During the fishing season you often see signs advertising *alose* for sale along this particular stretch of the river. Cadillac is a

The church of Verdelais is the last resting place
of artist Henri de Toulouse-Lautrec

*Vines are planted right up to the small church of
Loupiac, a village known for its dessert wines*

large fortified village with its fourteenth-century ramparts still intact. The
somewhat severe Château des Ducs d'Eperon sits high above the village, and
houses the Maison du Vin. Every Saturday, the village centre is closed to
traffic and a lively market is held in the streets and square.

From here, drive to Rions, a few kilometres to the north – it is surrounded
by medieval ramparts with a fortified gate, and has an old church and narrow
streets lined with crumbling stone houses. Just beyond the town is the ruined
Château de Langoiran; here a small road winds up past the château to the
hamlet of Haut-Langoiran, from where there are wonderful views down over
the vine-clad hill to the Gironde river and the countryside of Graves. The
village of Langoiran is set right beside the wide, rusty Garonne – it has a
riverside promenade and is a stopping-place for the barges which ply their
trade up and down the river to and from Bordeaux.

Now you can either cross back over the river and return towards Bordeaux
along the N 113, or you could extend your tour to include some of the
Premières Côtes de Bordeaux and Entre-Deux-Mers vineyards. This region,
which lies between the Garonne and Dordogne rivers, has a signposted circuit
through the countryside. Of particular interest is the majestic ruined
Romanesque abbey of la Sauve Majeure, an important stop for medieval
pilgrims following the Way of St James to Santiago de Compostella. Nearby
Créon is an interesting fortified town, and so are la Réole and Sauveterre-de-
Guyenne. But it is the unspoilt landscape and the quiet country roads that
meander through it that make this region a real pleasure.

A Case for Tasting

THE GRAVES REGION – named for its gravelly soil – runs south from the inner suburbs of Bordeaux down to the enchanted land that is Sauternes, where warm and misty autumns allow the long ripening of grapes for the world's greatest sweet wines. The Graves' own red wines, too, are among the finest of all.

CHÂTEAU DOISY-DAËNE

A *Deuxième Cru* at half the price of the likes of Guiraud, this excellent Barsac property's wines rival the very best of the entire region. The sweet white wine from the 1983 vintage is a classic, concentrated and luscious bottle. Good to drink young, but better after eight to ten years. 120FF.

CHÂTEAU GUIRAUD

Canadian-owned, this large estate is another of the élite *Premier Cru* properties of Sauternes. Guiraud neighbours the unrivalled Château d'Yquem (where prices are at least double that of any other Sauternes) and is in the process of adapting its production to compete with it. Guiraud vintages since that of 1983 are showing some modest success. 250FF.

CHÂTEAU LAFAURIE-PEYRAGUEY

One of 12 top-rated Sauternes properties, this relatively little-known wine fully earns its *Premier Cru Classé* status. Gorgeously intense in its honeyed, luscious flavour, the wine nevertheless has that paradoxical lightness and freshness that characterizes great Sauternes. The 1983 is superb. 250FF.

CHÂTEAU DES TOURS

Along with the *appellations* Cérons, Loupiac and Cadillac, Sainte-Croix-du-Mont produces sweet white wines that are, in effect, a low-cost alternative to Barsac and Sauternes. Des Tours is among the better properties, making a light wine with a good concentration of flavour. 30FF.

CHÂTEAU BASTOR-LAMONTAGNE

It is not only the *grands crus* of Barsac and Sauternes that provide delicious sweet white wines. For quality, this estate consistently matches the grandest, at a fraction of the price. Director Michel Garat justifiably enthuses about his wine's distinctive aromas of 'quince, oranges and spring flowers'. 60FF.

'R'

Several Sauternes properties make fine dry white wines. 'R' is a very good one, from the highly rated Rothschild-owned Château Rieussec. The wine has the enticing, honeyed scent of the sweet version, but the delicate, lemony-fresh flavour of dry white Bordeaux at its best. 60FF.

CHÂTEAU CHICANE

The Graves *appellation*'s southern tip, isolated from the mass of the district by Barsac and Sauternes, has a humble reputation. But the many properties of the south include some which make delicious claret at everyday prices. Chicane is medium-weight, with a 'smoky' flavour, for drinking young. 50FF.

DOMAINE DE GAILLAT

A southern Graves with real character. Usually made with 75% Cabernet Sauvignon grapes, this is a red wine to keep for three or four years, especially in good vintages such as 1985 and 1986. Juicy, blackcurranty wine that offers an introduction to the Graves style at a tenth of the price of Haut-Brion. 50FF.

CHÂTEAU MONTALIVET

The dry white wines of the Graves are the best of their kind from the entire Bordeaux region. Some are fabulously expensive; others, such as Montalivet – made from Semillon grapes and aged in new oak casks to give a rich and complex style – are comparative bargains. 50FF.

CHÂTEAU PAPE CLÉMENT

So-called after the archbishop whose home it was became Pope Clement V in 1305, this handsome property at Pessac in the Graves makes silky, lush red wine from the Cabernet Sauvignon (60%) and Merlot (40%) grapes alone. The good recent vintages such as 1982, 1983 and 1985 can be drunk after six years or so. 150FF.

CHÂTEAU HAUT-BRION

American-owned, and the greatest estate of the Graves, Haut-Brion was ranked *Premier Grand Cru Classé* in the famous 1855 classification of Bordeaux wines. Its claret, in great years such as 1978, 1982 and 1985, has been described as 'powerful and elegant', 'voluptuous' even 'monumental'. 400–500FF.

CHÂTEAU LA TOUR MARTILLAC

In common with other Graves estates, this property at Léognan in the southern reaches of the district, makes a very fine dry white wine – in this case exceptionally fruity and rich-tasting (80FF). The red is hearty and deep-flavoured, with the 'earthy' bouquet typical of Graves, and usually needs ten years' ageing. 70FF.

Cognac

Above: The vine-ribbed hillsides around the village of St Laurent
Left: The riverside warehouse of Hennessy in Cognac

*I*F CHAMPAGNE IS THE KING OF WINES, then cognac is certainly the emperor of *eau de vie*. It is more than just a type of brandy – it is the yardstick by which all others are measured. Brandy is simply a concentrated form of wine: when wine reaches an alcohol level of about 16 to 18 per cent during the fermentation process, the yeasts that transform the sugar into alcohol are killed off. For wine to be of greater strength than this, either pure alcohol must be added – as it is with port, for example – or it must be distilled to remove some of the water. This is how brandy is made – by heating wine to boiling point, then condensing the steam which it gives off.

In the Middle Ages the major exports from the Charente region were salt and wheat; the region's white wine was often only included in a shipment to complete the load. Later, in the seventeenth century, the wine-growers of Cognac began distilling their wines, partly in competition with growers closer to the coast, who had something of a monopoly in undistilled wine, and partly so that, in their more concentrated state, they could be shipped in greater quantities. On arrival in London or Amsterdam they were diluted with water before consumption. At this time brandy (from the Dutch *brandewijn*, or burnt wine), was not the choice of the gentry but a cheap, rough wine drunk by the proletariat as an alternative to beer.

THE WINES

The grape types used to make the wines from which cognac is distilled include the Saint-Emilion, a variety of Ugni Blanc, the Folle Blanche, the

Above: Vineyards near Segonzac
Right: The 12th-century Benedictine
abbey of Bassac
Previous pages: Summer sunlight and
riverside reflections near Juillac

Colombard, the Sauvignon and the Semillon. The process of distillation is quite complex and is carried on even today on small farms in the traditional copper stills. The thin and acidic white wines of Cognac, which are often little more than 8 to 10 per cent alcohol, are distilled in two stages to a strength of about 70 per cent alcohol. This is too strong and, immediately after distillation, too harsh to be drunk as it is. The fiery spirit is put into oak casks to mellow for at least two years – more for the finer cognacs. Its warm golden colour is a result of this process and of the tannin which it draws from the oak. Caramel may be added for colour and finally distilled water is used to dilute the spirit to its final strength of 40 per cent alcohol.

As well as cognac, this area produces *Pineau des Charentes*, which has its own appellation. This is an apéritif wine made by adding *eau de vie* to the white wine of the region; it is customarily served chilled. Some Vin de Pays is also produced with the name of *Vin de Pays des Charentes*.

THE CUISINE

The cuisine of the Cognac region benefits greatly from neighbouring Bordeaux and from Périgord to the east. Since it is close to the coast, good

seafood features on most menus. In *mouclade*, mussels are prepared with egg yolks, white wine and cream, while *chaudrée* is a fish stew in which a variety of fish and shellfish are cooked in a *court-bouillon* with white wine and shallots. Charentais melons are famous, with their firm, orangey-pink flesh and sweet, honey flavour. Here they are often prepared by slicing off the top, pouring in a good measure of Pineau des Charentes and leaving to chill slightly for a few hours before serving – they are wonderful!

THE ROUTE DES VINS *Michelin map 72*

The areas producing the wine from which cognac is made are divided into six *Crus*: Grande Champagne, Petite Champagne, Borderies, Fins Bois, Bons Bois and Bois Ordinaires: these last, lesser *Crus* are grown in regions as far away as the Ile de Ré and the Ile d'Oléron off the coast at La Rochelle, while the finer and more prestigious Grande Champagne is grown on the chalky hillsides south of the river Charente, near the town of Cognac itself. The suggested tour of the Cognac region is not signposted but it is easy to follow with the use of a map and includes the most significant of the Cognac villages and countryside.

Maize flourishing in front of the small, Romanesque church at Graves

A visit to Cognac is the ideal introduction to the region. It is a rather grey, grim-looking town, its roofs blackened by a fungus which thrives on the fumes emanating from the casks of maturing brandy. These casks are stored in the old part of the town, in riverside *chais* which you can visit; there is a regional museum here too, with a section on the making of cognac. Nearby are the Château de Valois, where François I was born in 1494, and the twelfth-century church of Saint Léger with its impressive Romanesque façade.

From the centre of Cognac take the N 141 towards Angoulême for a short distance and then turn left on to the D 15. Cross the river to the village of St Brice, which has a lovely sixteenth-century château set in a park. Nearby, close to Châtre, is the ruined twelfth-century Abbaye de Nôtre-Dame de Châtre, an elegant old stone building standing in isolation in the middle of a wood, surrounded by meadows and vineyards. Here, you are close to the lazy waters of the Charente, in a land of lush green water-meadows and woods and rolling hills of vineyards. You get a real sense of being far away from the rush and hurry of the twentieth century, particularly when you come to a town like Bourg-sur-Charente set beside an enchanting stretch of the river and dignified by a beautiful twelfth-century church and an imposing château that dates from the sixteenth century.

Jarnac, the next town on the circuit, is considered to be the second home of cognac; several important shippers are based here in riverside warehouses. The town has a broad, tree-lined main street and well cared for public gardens which stretch down to the river, as well as the château of Chabannes. The

A thatched stockpile of logs and vine prunings at St Médard-de-Barbezieux

peaceful little village of Triac also has a private château. From here, cross the Charente and take a small road, the D 90, to the village of St Même-les-Carrières, which is a good place for a walk by the river. In Bassac the Benedictine abbey, built in the twelfth century, has an unusual four-storey Romanesque bell tower and a fortified church. There are some handsome stone houses lining the narrow streets of the town. Another peaceful riverside spot lies at the point where the small road crosses the river at St Amant-de-Graves. Nearby Graves boasts an exquisite, small Romanesque church.

Everywhere you travel in the Cognac region you will see producers' farms. These are usually contained within high, grey stone walls behind large, closed doors, giving them a rather forbidding look. However, you will always be welcomed to taste the locally made cognac.

Châteauneuf-sur-Charente, further along the river, is somewhat larger than many of the other villages but quite similar in character; it has a fine twelfth-century Romanesque church. The route now turns away from the river to head back westward and begins to climb up into the chalky, domed hills where the vineyards are more densely cultivated. Between the small grey-stone village of Bouteville and its neighbour St Preuil, whose church is surrounded by vines, the road reaches the highest point of the undulating landscape, giving some fine views of the surrounding countryside. Nearby Lignières is a particularly charming village with a lovely Romanesque church and two châteaux: the moated seventeenth-century one is used as the town

hall, while the other is a newer building dating from the nineteenth century.

Beyond the tiny hamlets of Touzac and St Médard-de-Barbezieux, which has a quaint, tiny church in its centre, is Barbezieux, capital of the Petite Champagne region. This mellow old town has a network of narrow winding streets lined with old houses, a fine church and an imposing fifteenth-century château perched up above it all. There is yet another twelfth-century Romanesque church in the small village of Barret, next along the route. These churches are often quite tiny and have been so heavily restored that little of their original character remains. It is not uncommon to see fifteenth-century ribbed vaulting, a cloister that was added 200 years later and nineteenth-century marble cladding in a church dating from the Middle Ages. Beyond the town of Archiac, near St Fort-de-Né on the D 731, is a fine example of the region's dolmens (megalithic tombs), their mysterious stone formation looking rather incongruous in the middle of a vineyard.

The route turns eastwards from Archiac through the villages of Ambleville and Juillac-le-Coq and its twelfth-century church, through open countryside

*Above: The fortified gateway of Château
Chesnel where Cognac and Pineau
de Charentes may be sampled
Left: A sweeping view of the
vineyards from the road between
St Preuil and Bouteville*

that is a mixture of meadows, farmland, woods and vineyards. Around
Segonzac, the capital of the Grande Champagne region, the rounded chalk
hills are completely covered in neatly patterned vineyards, reminiscent of the
landscape in the Marne Valley where its aristocratic namesake is produced.

From here, you return towards Cognac through the small villages of Genté,
Gimeux and Ars, where there is a twelfth-century church and a Renaissance
château. The final part of the route leads through the villages of Merpins
(stop here to visit the remains of the Roman town of Condate and the mound
of a feudal castle), Jarnouzeau, Javrezac (beside the river Antenne) and
Richemont where there is a seventeenth-century château as well as an
eleventh-century one.

Before returning to Cognac it is worth travelling a little further to the north
to visit the twelfth-century Abbaye de Fontdouce near the town of Burie on
the D 73. On the way, just outside Cherves, is the fortified Château Chesnel,
the domain of the comtes de Roffignac, where you can sample and buy both
cognac and Pineau des Charentes.

A Case for Tasting

THE FIERY DELIGHTS OF COGNAC – appreciated overseas as much as in France itself – are purveyed by numerous famous, and countless not-so-famous, *maisons*. Each firm typically offers half a dozen different grades from basic three-star to deluxe XO (extra old). Here are just a few of them.

HINE

Dorset-born teenager Thomas Hine was in the cognac town of Jarnac to learn French when the Revolution closed France's borders in 1792. So he made the best of it – and founded the revered firm his great-great-great grandsons run today. Hine VSOP Fine Champagne is beautifully smooth and aromatic. 120FF.

MARTELL

Founded by Channel Islander Jean Martell in 1715, this Cognac giant has more than 100,000 oak casks of brandy slumbering to maturity in its sprawl of buildings in the town. Martell cognacs have a distinctive mellowness. The three-star is blended from five- to seven-year-old brandies. 90FF.

BISQUIT

Based outside Cognac at Lignères, the Bisquit estate of nearly 500 acres is the largest in the region, and supplies about a sixth of the vast, modern distillery's needs. The three-star is a deliciously fruity young brandy. 'The youth of the spirit,' Bisquit rightly claim, 'has an attractive vigour which older styles lose.' 80FF.

OTARD

A descendant of the Scottish Otard family bought the Château de Cognac, the town's massively fortified centrepiece, in the midst of the Revolution in 1795 – and found it an ideal place in which to mature brandy. It still serves the purpose. Otard VSOP Fine Champagne is 'subtle, full-bodied with a pronounced bouquet'. 120FF.

DELAMAIN

This firm produces only old brandies. Delamain Pale & Dry is indeed light in colour, but gloriously intense in flavour – very fine cognac. It is blended entirely from Grande Champagne cognacs of 25 or more years old. The firm has been family-owned since its foundation by Irishman James Delamain in 1759. 270FF.

ROULLET

Part-owned by a British brewery, this family firm produces very fine old brandies largely from its own vineyards. Extra Grande Champagne, aged more than 15 years in oak, is a lovely dark cognac with a rich, raisiny scent and a lingeringly delicious, ardent flavour. 250FF.

ROFFIGNAC

At the splendid Renaissance-style Château Chesnel just north of Cognac, the Roffignac family have been small-scale producers for more than a century. Roffignac Napoléon is a blend of brandies from the Chesnel estate and from Grande Champagne with a minimum age of 12 years. 200FF.

HENNESSY

Cognac's biggest firm sells less than 5 per cent of its brandy in France – the legacy of an Irish founder (in 1765) primarily intent on exports. Hennessy Fine Champagne VSOP, so known because it is blended entirely from brandies of the Grande and Petite Champagne districts, includes spirit up to 25 years old. 120FF.

COURVOISIER

'*Le Cognac de Napoléon*' since the founder, Emmanuel Courvoisier, supplied Bonaparte's imperial court in the early 1800s, this famous firm makes exceptionally rich, smooth cognacs. Courvoisier XO is surely the *dernier mot*: dark amber in colour, rich, complex aroma and enormously flavoursome – blended from brandies up to 60 years old. 400FF.

PHILIPPE DE CASTAIGNE PINEAU DES CHARENTES

Numerous Cognac companies make Pineau, which now has its own *appellation contrôlée* and must be made with Charentais grapes (mainly Ugni Blanc) whose fermentation is stopped by the addition of cognac. As with all *pineaux*, Castaigne's sweet but palate-stimulating version should be served well chilled. 40FF.

JULES ROBIN PINEAU DES CHARENTES

The *apéritif* of the Cognac region was, so the story goes, discovered by a 16th-century *vigneron* who mistakenly poured some newly pressed grape juice into a barrel containing a little cognac. Years passed and *voilà*, the clear, sweet fortified wine was the happy result. Jules Robin is a best-seller. 40FF.

VIN DE PAYS DES CHARENTES

Most of the Cognac region's wine goes, not unnaturally, into the distilleries, but some survives as *vin de pays*. The reds and rosés are rather acid, but the whites can have a good measure of fruitiness to balance the sharpness. Refreshing, light and dry wine usually sold as low-cost 'own-label' brands. 10FF.

Bergerac

Above: Tasting the wares at the wine fair of Sigoules
Left: A country cottage near St Laurent des Vignes

YRANO DE BERGERAC, the legendary figure created by the nineteenth-century dramatist Edmond Rostand, was a romantic hero from a tormented past. Thus is the city of Bergerac, situated beside the Dordogne on a broad plain where the river makes its way towards the wide Gironde Estuary, inscribed in French literature. It is less famous for its wines, undeservedly so. Only 85 kilometres away from the city of Bordeaux and with the western limits of its vineyards virtually adjoining those of the Libournais, Bergerac tends to be almost ignored. But its wines are worth exploring, particularly the sweet white wine of Monbazillac. The city of Bergerac has a fascinating old quarter with narrow cobbled streets and medieval houses and courtyards and a Maison du Vin. Tobacco is an important product of the region too – indeed, you can follow a Route des Tabacs as well as the Route des Vins.

THE WINES

The wines of Bergerac, red, white and some rosé, are sold under the following appellations: *Bergerac* (red, white and rosé); *Côtes de Bergerac* (red and white); *Bergerac-Côtes de Saussagnac* (white); *Monbazillac* (white); *Montravel, Côtes de Montravel* and *Haut Montravel* (white); *Pécharmant* (red), and *Rosette* (white). The grape types used are principally the Cabernet Franc, Cabernet Sauvignon, Merlot, Cot (or Malbec), Semillon and Sauvignon Blanc.

Monbazillac is probably the best-known wine of the region. It is sweet and white, and can be drunk chilled as an apéritif, as an accompaniment to *foie gras*

*The 15th-century Château de Bridoire, a short distance
to the south of Monbazillac*

or as a dessert wine. As with the great sweet wines of neighbouring Sauternes and Barsac, Monbazillac is made from grapes affected by the Botrytis fungus.

THE CUISINE

The neighbouring region of Périgord has a strong influence on the cuisine of the Bergerac region. *Pâté de foie gras* studded with truffles is an expensive treat; it is perfect with a glass of golden Monbazillac wine. Walnuts are a major crop here: walnut oil is used as a dressing on salads, and you'll often see walnut bread served with the cheese. There is a superb *boulangerie*, Michel de Queker, in Ste Foy-la-Grande where you will find this as well as breads with onions, with raisins or prunes, soda bread and wholemeal bread, pastries – including croissants with ham and cheese – *croques-monsieurs* and *madames*, quiches and sweet pastries like *clafoutis*, and apple, greengage and grape tart.

THE ROUTES DES VINS *Michelin map 75*

The Bergerac Route des Vins is a complete, if meandering, circuit and is well signposted. It is also particularly well planned. If you leave by the bridge near the old quarter and cross over to the south bank of the Dordogne, you will pick up the signposts, starting on the D 933, the main road to Marmande. Very soon the Route des Vins turns left on a small country road, the D 14, towards Monbazillac. As you drive over the wide Dordogne plain you can see in the distance the large rounded hill where most of the southerly vineyards are situated. The Moulin de Malfourat, an old windmill, now without its sails, provides a superb viewpoint over the sloping vineyards leading down to the

The vine-patterned slopes which spread out below the village of Monbazillac

*The 16th-century Château of Monbazillac, now owned by the
Cave-Co-opérative*

Above: Carefully picking the grapes
which are coated with 'noble rot'
in the vineyards of Pomport
near Monbazillac
Right: The early calm of a
summer morning below the old
bridge of Ste Foy-la-Grande

Dordogne Valley and the distant town of Bergerac.

There is not much of interest in Monbazillac itself, an unassuming cluster of grey stone houses around a small square. But stop at the adjacent château, an elegant and successful mixture of Renaissance and military architecture dating from the sixteenth century. It has *caves* you can visit, and a restaurant. Now you are in the heart of vineyard country. Leave the wine road for a short detour to the nearby fifteenth-century Château de Bridoire. Then continue through the small villages of Rouffignac-de-Sigoulès and Pomport on a small winding country road towards Sigoulès, which holds an annual wine fair in July. Next to it is the tiny village of Monbos with its miniature grey stone, turreted château. Little more than a rough track leads to the village. Certainly this wine route includes the quietest and most scenic small roads wherever possible. Cycling would be an ideal form of transport here.

The countryside becomes flatter, and more open now and the vines alternate with meadows and woods. The small road continues to the hamlet of Thénac; you can taste the local wines at Château Thénac. A sequence of minute villages follows: la Bastide, Monestier and Gageac-et-Rouillac, where there is an attractive fourteenth-century château. Saussignac, the next village, is rather larger, with an imposing château. Now you head back towards the River Dordogne to the busy market town of Ste Foy-la-Grande, an ancient *bastide*. Here the route crosses the river to Port Ste-Foy, where it turns left on to the D 32 E 2 towards Vélines in the region of Montravel. The village has a lovely Romanesque church and mellow, old, grey stone houses.

From here the wine road continues to Moncaret and Lamothe-Montravel, where there is the large Cave Co-opérative of Montravel. The small village of St Michel-de-Montaigne is the next place of interest on the route; there is an

The Château of St Michel-de-Montaigne, rebuilt after a fire which destroyed the former home of the 16th-century French essayist

old Romanesque church here and a château which you can visit and where you can buy the wines made in the surrounding vineyards. The circuit continues along a small scenic road through woods and meadows towards Montpeyroux, which also has a fine old church and a château, the Manoir de Mathecoulon. You are in the Côtes de Bergerac region now – the western limit of the Bergerac vineyards and close to the wine-producing area of St Emilion. Next is the *bastide* town of Villefranche-de-Lonchat with a nice old

church, a pretty square shaded by plane trees, and a Cave Co-opérative. The lake of Gurson, a peaceful spot where there is a restaurant under the trees, is nearby; it has camping, picnic and boating facilities, and is overlooked by the ruined Château de Gurson.

From here the Route des Vins continues back towards Ste Foy-la-Grande through some small, unremarkable villages. After passing St Méard-de-Gurçon on the main road (the D 708), the wine road turns left on to a small, country road leading to the hamlet of Ponchapt. Towards the town of le Fleix, as the road descends to the river, there are occasional views through the trees of the valley below. From here it returns to Bergerac along the D 32.

Route des vins signs near Monbazillac

The regions of Pécharmant and Rosette lie to the north and east of Bergerac and, although not part of the signposted wine route, are well worth exploring. Take the main road, the N 21, towards Périgueux from the centre of Bergerac. After the village of Lembras you will find the D 21 to the right leading to the little village of Lamonzie-Montastruc, which boasts the Château de Bellegarde and the Manoir de Grateloup.

To the south-east of the riverside village of Mouleydier is Lanquais, where you can visit the very fine fifteenth-century château. There is another château in Bannes, and the medieval town of Issigeac is of interest too with a sixteenth-century church and a bishops' palace, le Château des Evêques, built a century later, as well as some picturesque old timber-framed houses.

If you want to extend your visit to Bergerac further, you can follow the Circuit des Bastides, a shortish tour which takes you to many of the ancient *bastide* towns in the region, such as Beaumont, Villeréal, Eymet and, perhaps the greatest jewel, Montpazier, which is no great distance from the thriving vineyards of Monbazillac.

To the south-west of Bergerac is the small wine-growing region of the Côtes de Duras, where excellent red and white wines are made; if you have the time it is worth a short detour. The town of Duras, almost due south of Ste Foy-la-Grande, has a château housing an intriguing museum of regional agricultural implements and domestic bric-à-brac, including ancient wine presses and bottles. The countryside is tranquil and the people welcoming, and it is a pleasure to drive slowly through the small villages scattered among the vineyards, such as St Sernin and St Théobald.

Vineyards near Thénac at the southern extremity of the Bergerac wine region

*The 17th-century Château de Duras, now housing a
museum of traditional crafts and artifacts*

A Case for Tasting

IN BERGERAC AND NEIGHBOURING DURAS AND BUZET, enterprising *vignerons* make fine wines in the style of the big names of Bordeaux – but at far more approachable prices. Strict *appellation contrôlée* laws, combined with improved technology mean that these are now some of the most interesting of all France's 'country' wines.

CHÂTEAU COURT-LES-MÛTS

Another Bergerac property with a good name for all its wines. Court-Les-Mûts makes a very fine rosé from Cabernet Sauvignon grapes, the dark skins of which are left in with the newly pressed juice just long enough to impart a deep pink colour. Fragrant wine with a ripe, lingering flavour. 30FF.

BUZET BARON D'ARDEUIL

This is the flagship red wine of the Buzet co-op. Previously known as Cuvée Napoléon the wine is deeply flavoured, dark and sweet-smelling, with the vanilla character of oak-ageing. The 1986 is a classic, for drinking from the early 1990s. 30FF.

CHÂTEAU LA JAUBERTIE

British owned and run – by a member of the Ryman family, of stationery shop fame – La Jaubertie produces an outstanding range of Bergerac wines. The Cépage Sauvignon is a mouthwateringly fresh and fruity dry white with a spring-flower scent. 30FF.

CÔTES DE DURAS SEIGNEURET

Another co-op Duras, this time from the *producteurs réunis* at Landerrouat. This is a juicy red wine that compares well with grander-sounding Bordeaux appellation wines. Serve young Duras reds slightly cool, rather than at room temperature, to make the most of their freshness. 10FF.

BUZET VIGNERONS RÉUNIS

The big co-operative at Buzet-sur-Baize produces the bulk of the district's wine – and to very high standards. The basic red Buzet lives honourably up to the co-op's claim of 'supple, balanced and finely scented' wine. Plenty of fruit and a pleasing 'grassy' character. 20FF.

CHÂTEAU LA BORDERIE

Bergerac reds cannot compete for quality with their neighbours to the west in St Emilion, but they do represent good value. La Borderie is a medium-bodied but complex wine which makes good drinking after four or five years' ageing. 30FF.

CHÂTEAU DE TIREGAND

The tiny Pécharmant *appellation* lies at Bergerac's east end, and produces red wines very much in the classic Bordeaux style. Tiregand's wines are rich and deep-flavoured with the 'elegant' harmony of flavour that characterizes good St Emilion. Best after five years' ageing. 40FF.

CHÂTEAU DU TREUIL DE NAILHAC

A very good Monbazillac property making truly luscious but cleanly fresh wine of real character. It is best served very cold, but as an *apéritif* or with a rich starter such as *foie gras*, rather than with a dessert. In good years, when the autumn has been warm and the grapes picked late (1983 and 1986, for example) Du Treuil makes wine to keep ten years. 40FF.

CHÂTEAU MONBAZILLAC

A visit to the grand Renaissance château – built nevertheless in nostalgically medieval style – at Monbazillac is *de rigueur* on any tour of the region. The wine, made by the Monbazillac co-operative, is on sale at the château, and of good, if sometimes unexceptional, quality. 40FF.

CHÂTEAU DES JONQUILLES

The grapes for the red wines of the increasingly respected Côtes de Buzet appellation are Cabernet Sauvignon, Cabernet Franc, Merlot and Malbec – very much the Bordeaux formula. The small Jonquilles estate's wine, however, is 100 per cent Merlot. A mellow and untypical Buzet. 30FF.

CÔTES DE DURAS LES PRODUCTEURS RÉUNIS

Duras makes something of a speciality of supplying high-quality, low-cost wines for bulk export. This slurpable red, made from the classic Bordeaux grapes, comes from the co-op at St Laurent des Vignes – also the source of a good dry white Sauvignon. 10FF.

CHÂTEAU SEPTY

Monbazillac, like Pécharmant, is an appellation within the Bergerac district. Its wines are all of the 'dessert' variety – sweet and white. The grapes used are Sauvignon and Semillon (as in Sauternes) plus a little Muscadelle. Septy makes rich but clean-tasting wine to drink young. 40FF.

Wine-buying Guide

This part of the region produces a great volume of wine, most of which is not well known. The wines here are relatively unaffected by the investment market that has caused prices for the top wines to spiral, and so, apart from the top wines of St Emilion and Pomerol, most fetch modest prices.

APPELLATIONS CONTRÔLÉES
St Emilion This appellation has its own classification system for red wines:
St Emilion, *Premier Grand Cru Classé* – the top chateaux
St Emilion, *Grand Cru Classé* – about 70 châteaux
St Emilion, *Grand Cru* – fixed annually by official tasting panels.

Here the Merlot is the dominant red grape variety and makes generally softer wines than in the Médoc. The wines of a good year from the better chateaux need five to ten years' ageing, but the lesser wines are drinkable after two or three.

The village itself, surrounded by the vineyards, is one of the most beautiful wine villages in France. Fortunately, many growers have had their homes converted into *caves*.

Around St Emilion are satellite appellations that append the name of St Emilion. They are all red wines of a lesser standing than St Emilion itself: Lussac-St

Left: The Château de Monbazillac

Emilion, Montagne-St Emilion, Puisseguin-St Emilion, Saint-Georges-St Emilion.

Since 1973 all the wines of Parsac-St Emilion have been sold as Montagne-St Emilion.

Pomerol A small appellation north-east of Libourne producing rich, sturdy red wines. Again, the Merlot is the predominant grape variety here. The estates are all quite small by Bordeaux standards and there is no official classification system. However, Château Pétrus is acknowledged as being by far the best. It is the most expensive wine not only of Bordeaux, but in the entire world.

Lalande-de-Pomerol A satellite appellation to Pomerol making similar but less rich red wines.

Néac A tiny appellation next to Lalande-de-Pomerol making similar red wines.

Fronsac An appellation producing soft, rich red wines similar to Pomerol, that has somehow always missed the limelight enjoyed by Pomerol and St Emilion. A second appellation, Canon Fronsac, exists for similar red wines in the same delimited area.

Côtes de Blaye, Premières Côtes de Blaye Some dry to sweet white wines but mostly red of a rustic and soft nature. The best vineyards for the red are by the River Gironde. The Premières

Côtes de Blaye is from the same district but is required to have an extra half degree of alcohol.

Bourg and *Côtes de Bourg* A much smaller appellation area adjacent and very similar to Blaye.

Côtes de Castillon Red wines from just west of St Emilion. This appellation is technically a Bordeaux Supérieur and produces good value wines.

Graves de Vayres A small appellation, not to be confused with Graves, making red, dry white, and demi-sec white wine all to be drunk young.

Entre-deux-Mers A large appellation area that used to produce sweet white wines but now is only allowed to produce drier styles. It should be drunk young and is a good value *apéritif*. Red wines produced in this area are designated Bordeaux or Bordeaux Supérieur.

Premières Côtes de Bordeaux Some red and *clairet* (rosé) wines but the white, ranging from dry to sweet, is best known. Most of the wines are inexpensive and good value.

Sainte-Foy-Bordeaux The extreme eastern appellation of Bordeaux, bordering Bergerac, making red and dry to sweet white wines.

Côtes de Bordeaux Saint-Macaire Sweet or semi-sweet white wine normally drunk young.

The vineyards and Château de Cos d'Estournel in the Médoc

THE MEDOC

This vineyard district commands worldwide attention from both wine lovers and the investment market. Most of the greater châteaux are not geared up to welcome tourist visitors, especially those without an appointment, and will anyway have tied up arrangements for selling their wine through brokers and *négociants*.

During the normal holiday months, May to September, the two preceding vintages will be undergoing their early maturation in oak casts. Most properties will allow visitors to sample wines from the cask but bear in mind that they will be nowhere near ready for drinking, and the *maître de chais* may be pressed for time. Therefore, you

might like to have these guidelines:

■ have some knowledge of the past three or four vintages and be able to discuss them in French;
■ don't visit between 12 and 2 pm unless you have been asked to

■ don't smoke in the *chais*. Never pour wine left in your sampling glass back into the cask
■ be courteous, shake hands and comment briefly on the wines you have tasted without wasting the *maître de chais'* time

The châteaux that do sell directly are well aware of the tourist market and charge accordingly. It might be better to buy wines in Bordeaux town centre from the Vinothèque shop at the end of the Allées de Tourny opposite the theatre.

THE APPELLATIONS
The generic wines are sold as Médoc and Haut-Médoc, both of which only cover red wines.

The Haut-Médoc is subdivided into communes which all have their own appellations: Listrac, Moulis, Margaux, St Julien, Pauillac and St Estèphe.

Within these commune appellations there are châteaux rated on the classification scale of *Grand Cru* (a scale set out in 1855 with five divisions), *Cru*

Bourgeois, Cru Artisan and *Cru Paysan*.

THE 1855 GRAND CRU CLASSIFICATION

This classification was formed by the Bordeaux Chamber of Commerce on the instructions of Napoleon III for the *Exposition Universelle de Paris*. It was based on

the price fetched per *tonneau* of wine in 1855.

Since the original classification some châteaux have fallen into relative disrepute, while others have gained in stature, making the system rather inaccurate in parts. Nevertheless, it still provides a loose guide to quality.

In 1855 four châteaux were rated *Premier Grand Cru Classé*: Château Lafite in Pauillac, Château Latour also in Pauillac, Château Margaux in Margaux and Château Haut-Brion in Graves.

Although Graves is not normally considered as part of the Médoc, Haut-Brion is nevertheless universally recognized and classified as a *Premier Grand Cru*.

In 1973 a presidential decree elevated Château Mouton-Rothschild (in Pauillac) to a *Premier Grand Cru* so there are now five. There are also 14 *Deuxième Grand Cru* châteaux, 14 *Troisièmes Crus*, ten *Quatrièmes Crus* and 18 *Cinquièmes Crus*.

THE SOUTHERN BORDELAIS

This area starts within the suburbs of Bordeaux itself and stretches south-eastwards. The best Graves estates of Château Haut-Brion, La Mission-Haut-Brion and La Tour-Haut-Brion are, quite surprisingly, in the built-up area of Pessac.

APPELLATIONS CONTRÔLÉES

Graves This appellation produces red and dry to demi-sec white wines. The quality ranges from a *Premier Grand Cru*, Château Haut-Brion, through a succession of

Grand Cru Classé châteaux, down to the basic commune wine, Graves. An appellation of *Graves Supérieures* exists for commune white wine, ranging from dry to sweet, with an extra degree of alcohol.

Sauternes This appellation produces only sweet white wine made from grapes infected by the Botrytis fungus. This rich, luscious wine is the most perfect accompaniment for puddings or *foie gras*. In some years the ripeness and effect of the Botrytis is better than others and makes richer, more concentrated wines that will last and improve over time.

Barsac Again, a sweet white wine from Botrytis-infected grapes but marginally lighter than Sauternes. All Barsac is entitled to be called Sauternes but not *vice versa*.

Cérons This appellation, adjacent to Barsac, also makes sweet white wines from grapes infected by the Botrytis fungus, but makes dry wines as well. The wines are less rich than Barsac or Sauternes and do not last as long.

Loupiac and Cadillac Opposite Cérons on the right bank of the Garonne, these two adjacent appellations make semi-sweet to sweet white wines of which Loupiac is the richer.

Sainte-Croix-du-Mont Sweet white wines are produced here next to Loupiac. Some wine is made dry to be sold as Bordeaux *sec*, but most has a lemony lusciousness.

Vineyards near Segonzac in the Grande Champagne region of Cognac

The wines are well made and provide a cheaper, less intense alternative to Sauternes or Barsac.

BORDEAUX

GENERAL BORDEAUX APPELLATIONS

Bordeaux is the biggest AC region in France, with a massive production and several large generic appellations covering lower quality wines.

Bordeaux Red, dry or sweet white, and rosé wines from any part of the Bordeaux region. The dry white wines must state *sec* on the label. These wines are more likely to be blends made by *négociants* than to come from a single estate.

Bordeaux Clairet An appellation to cover wines that are light red/dark rosé. The English word Claret is a corruption of this name. This is the original style of Bordeaux red wine but now is only really found on estates where they produce it for home consumption.

Bordeaux Mousseux The sparkling *méthode champenoise* wine that can be dry to *demi-sec*.

Bordeaux Rosé Dry rosé wine, not common.

Bordeaux Supérieur Red, dry to sweet white, and rosé wine that is the same as generic Bordeaux except that it has an extra degree of alcohol, and comes only from the more noble grape varieties.

COGNAC

This is a much-copied name, often used to describe grape brandy. In fact it is the spirit from this delimited region. Within the Cognac district there are six sub-districts: Grande Champagne, Petite Champagne, Borderies, Fins Bois, Bons Bois and Bois Ordinaires, in order of quality. The quality of the spirit depends on the chalk content of the soil.

Commercial cognac houses blend spirits from all or just a few of the districts to make their house styles. Three-star is the basic quality designation,

requiring the spirit to be aged for a minimum of two years in Limousin oak barrels. VSOP (Very Special Old Pale) must have a minimum of three years' ageing but in practice both three star and VSOP are invariably aged longer. Five years is now the maximum age allowed to be stated on a label, however old the blend of spirits is. Most houses produce a de-luxe blend that contains a proportion of old, long-aged spirits but the packaging undoubtedly adds to the expense. Vintage cognacs do exist and you may be able to buy them from a merchant at home with old stocks, but they are now outlawed in France so do not expect to see any there.

On the other side of the coin there are many small growers and producers (*fermiers*) who make a less blended, perhaps finer cognac that enthusiasts often prefer. Do not expect to see very much at these smaller firms, but you will probably find it interesting to taste the drink and hear their philosophies on cognac. When tasting, smell the spirit with your nose an inch from the glass. Don't stick your nose right into the glass or the fumes will anaesthetize your sense of smell.

To get a balanced view of cognac, try to spend some time with producers of alternative cognacs such as M. Voisin of Léopold Gourmel.

Pineau des Charentes This is a Vin Doux Naturel, used as an *apéritif* and fortified to about 17°. It has not caught on abroad but is well worth a try.

VIN DE PAYS
Vin de Pays des Charentes Red, dry white and rosé wines of which the whites are the best, from the *departements* of Charente and Charente-Maritime.

BERGERAC

The vineyards start immediately to the east of the city of Bordeaux. Most of the wines are fairly ordinary ones in the Bordeaux style, but there are appellations within the generic Bergerac AC that make interesting wines.

APPELLATIONS CONTRÔLÉES
Bergerac This generic appellation covers the red and less interesting rosé wines. A separate AC, Bergerac Sec, exists for the dry white wine made primarily from Sauvignon grapes. The sweet whites are called *moëlleux*.

Côtes de Bergerac Superior red wines with an extra degree of alcohol produced in the same area as Bergerac.

Côtes de Bergerac-Côtes de Saussignac A dry white wine from five communes around Saussignac.

Pécharmant This is a better red wine produced in the north-eastern part of Bergerac, with one degree more alcohol than straight Bergerac.

Monbazillac An appellation within Bergerac that produces sweet white wine. Although these wines are made with Botrytis-infected grapes, similar to nearby Sauternes, they do not achieve the richness of Sauternes. The wine can be drunk young or up to four years' ageing and is very good value. In good years it can be kept longer.

Rosette A semi-sweet white wine from north of Bergerac. It is not very common, and most is drunk locally.

Montravel An appellation technically within the *enclave* of Bordeaux but actually in the *département* of Dordogne. Dry, *demi-sec* and sweet white wines are made under the name Montravel and the reds are sold as Bergerac. Côtes de Montravel-Haut-Montravel also exists within Montravel.

Côtes de Duras Red and dry and sweet white wines made in western Bergerac. The wines are in the Bordeaux style and can be quite attractive as well as good value.

Côtes de Buzet This appellation makes red, dry white and rosé wines of quite good quality. Most of the production is from the Cave Co-opérative at Buzet-sur-Baise where they have a prestige red wine called Baron d'Ardeuil aged in new oak casks. The rosé production is tiny.

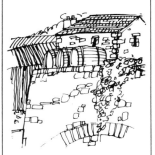

VDQS
Côtes du Marmandais Although only VDQS status, these red and dry white wines are well made and good value. The reds are the best.

An enthusiast at the annual wine fair in Sigoules, Bergerac

Museums and Châteaux

BORDEAUX

Some Bordeaux properties are very much better equipped to welcome visitors than others. Those that do will usually offer a tour of the *chais* (ground-floor cellars) where wines are fermented and cask-aged. You may be able to taste young wine from the wood. Tours may extend, too, to the vineyards, but as many châteaux are in fact private homes, do not expect to see over the house.

MAISON DU VIN DE BORDEAUX

The right starting point for visiting châteaux, as this is the headquarters of the Bordeaux wine trade's association, offering information, tours and visits to particular estates. Tastings of a wide range of the region's wines are also offered here.
1 Cours du 30 Juillet, 33075 Bordeaux.
Tel (56) 44–28–41.
Open Mon–Fri, 9am–5pm; Sat pm only.

CHÂTEAU DE LA RIVIÈRE

'My experienced staff and I will be pleased to show you the estate – even if you buy nothing,' says the splendidly moustachioed owner of this beautiful Fronsac château, Jacques Borie. He suggests you 'reserve 1½–2 hours for your visit'.
St Michel de Fronsac, 33126 Fronsac.
Tel (57) 24–98–01.
Open Mon–Fri, 8–11am and 2–5pm.

CHÂTEAU SOUTARD

An elegant St Emilion estate making sublime wines to rival the best of the region. The château is a masterpiece of 18th-century architecture, as impeccably maintained as the wines are impeccably made. Tastings offered. It is vital to telephone for an appointment.
33330 St Emilion.
Tel (57) 51–72–23.
Open Mon–Fri, 8am–12 noon and 3–7pm.

VIEUX CHÂTEAU CERTAN

Oldest of the Pomerol estates, the château is a modest but beautifully proportioned 19th-century building in the *chartreuse* style.
Pomerol, 33500 Libourne.
Tel (57) 51–17–33.
Visits by appointment only.

CHÂTEAU MOUTON-ROTHSCHILD

One of the great showpieces of the Médoc, this *Premier Grand Cru Classé* of the Pauillac commune incorporates a wonderful *Musée du Vin*. Not to be missed.
33250 Pauillac.
Tel (56) 59–22–22.
Open Mon–Fri, 9.30–11.30am and 2–5pm. By appointment only in July, Sept and Oct; closed Aug.

CHÂTEAU CISSAC

A modest Médoc estate centred on a large, idyllic house and *chais* dating from 1769. Visitors are made very welcome at this family domain, where they made outstanding wines in the 1982, 1983 and 1985 vintages.
Cissac–Médoc, 33250 Pauillac.
Tel (56) 59–58–39.
Open Mon–Fri, 9am–12noon and 2–5pm.

CHÂTEAU PRIEURÉ-LICHINE

Stop off to buy a bottle or two of the lovely wine made at this *Quatrième Grand Cru Classé* in Margaux, and you are likely to find yourself doing business with the owner, Alexis Lichine. He is one of the leading members of the Bordeaux trade and, as you

will find, a very keen promoter of his own wines!
33460 Margaux.
Tel (56) 88–36–28.
Open daily 9am–7pm.

CHÂTEAU HAUT-BRION

In its pleasing fairy-tale style, the turreted castle – parts of which date back to the 1500s – presides over the oldest and greatest estate of the Graves region.
BP 24, 33600 Pessac-Cedex.
Tel (56) 98–28–17.
Open, by appointment only, Mon–Fri, 8–11.30am and 2–5pm.

CHÂTEAU DE MALLE

Pepperpot towers flank this superb 17th-century Sauternes château, ancestral home of the Comtes de Bournazel. A very good, middle-priced sweet wine is made here, but de Malle's main interest is that it is a historic monument filled with art treasures. There is a fine Italian garden and much romantic statuary.
Preignac, 33210 Langon.
Tel (56) 63–28–67.
Château open Easter to 15 Oct daily except Wed, 3–6pm.

COGNAC

The famous cognac houses are well accustomed to visitors from all parts of the world, and offer

Early morning sunlight melts the September mist at the Château de Monbazillac

Springtime in the water meadows of the Charente near Jarnac

interesting tours of their distilleries and warehouses – where the spirits age in cask, each year losing through evaporation the few per cent of their precious contents charmingly known as the 'angels' share'.

MUSÉE DU COGNAC

As well as exhibitions devoted to the long history of the great brandy, there are important archaeological and other collections devoted to the region.
Boulevard Denfert-Rochereau, 16100 Cognac.
Tel tourist office for details (45) 82–10–71.
Open June–Sept daily except Tue, 10am–12 noon and 2–5.30pm; Oct–May daily except Tue, 2–5.30pm only.

COURVOISIER

The very grand Château Courvoisier, built on the site of a 15th-century fort on the river Charente at Jarnac, has its own museum dedicated to cognac and to Napoleon – one of Courvoisier's first customers.
Place du Château, 16200 Jarnac.
Tel (45) 35–55–55.
Telephone to check tour times.

LÉOPOLD GOURMEL

Owner Pierre Voisin blends and matures the cognacs for his small, independent business with idiosyncratic skill and infectious enthusiasm.
BP 194, 16016 Cognac.
Tel (45) 82–07–29.
By appointment only.

MARTELL

Three thousand growers supply the mountains of grapes for this cognac giant, whose vast premises in the town make a fascinating tour. Allow about an hour for the visit and the free tastings.
Place Edouard–Martell, 16100 Cognac.
Tel (45) 82–44–44.

by the Black Prince – this picturesque enterprise now receives 50,000 visitors a year.
Château de Cognac, 16100 Cognac.
Tel (45) 82–40–40.
Open Oct 1–Mar 31, Mon–Fri. Tours at 10 and 11am and 2, 3, 4 and 5pm.

ROFFIGNAC

A range of cognacs and *pineaux des charentes* are on sale at the handsome, Italianate château and visitors see an audiovisual show as well as the stills and *chais.*
Château Chesnel, 16370 Cherves de Cognac, Richemont.
Tel (45) 83–28–11.
Open daily.

BERGERAC

Rather overshadowed by the grandeur of Bordeaux, this region's châteaux nevertheless have great style of their own.

MUSÉE DU VIN ET DE LA BATELLERIE

Bergerac's momentous regional history as well as its long winemaking tradition are celebrated in the modest museum.
5 Rue des Conférences, 24100 Bergerac.
Tel tourist office (53) 57–03–11 for opening times according to season.

CHÂTEAU DE MONBAZILLAC

The majestic castle, built in the middle of the 16th century, brims

with fine antique furniture, tapestries and other treasures and has its own museum devoted to the region's wines. One of the original *chais* has been converted into a restaurant.
Monbazillac 24240.
Tel (53) 57–06–38.
Open daily, Oct–Apr, 10am–12 noon and 2.30–5pm; May, 9.30am–12 noon and 2–6pm; Jun–Sept, 9.30am–12.30pm and 2–7.30pm.

CHÂTEAU LA JAUBERTIE

Local lore has it that this large and handsome villa, built around 1800 onto the ruins of a 16th-century house, began life as the secret *rendezvous* of a prosperous local doctor and his mistress – inevitably, a dancer. Today the charming home of Englishman Nick Ryman and his family, the château offers tastings and direct sales of the estate's exceptional wines.
Colombier, 24560 Issigeac.
Tel (53) 58-32-11.
Open daily for tasting, 8am–12 noon and 2–6pm.

LES VIGNERONS RÉUNIS DES CÔTES DE BUZET

The Buzet co-operative welcomes visitors and offers direct sales of the excellent range of wines at attractive prices. There is an audiovisual display, small wine-and-vine museum, and free tastings.
Buzet-sur-Baize, 47160 Damazan.
Tel (53) 84–74–30.
Open daily, 9am–12 noon and 2–6pm.

Open July and Aug, Mon–Sat, 8.30–11am and 2–5pm; 1 Sept–30 Jun, Mon–Fri, 8.30–11am and 2–5pm (Fri am only except June and Sept).

OTARD

Established since 1795 in the historic Château de Cognac – which retains vestiges of the 13th-century castle often visited

Gastronomic Specialities

A LA BORDELAISE on a menu usually signifies a dish simmered in the wine of the region, red or white. The shallots that flourish in the local river valleys are an important ingredient in the sauce base – finely chopped and sautéed in oil and butter. Look out for **ENTRECÔTE À LA BORDELAISE** (with beef marrow) and the exotic **ÉCREVISSES BORDELAISES** (crayfish).

AGNEAU DE PAUILLAC, from sheep pastured on the shores of the Gironde, is a prized local meat said to be the perfect complement to claret.

LAMPROIE The strange, spineless eel-like fish of the Gironde estuary, the lamprey is traditionally cooked **À LA BORDELAISE** to produce a flavour one gastronomic writer describes as 'between that of turbot and rabbit'.

GRAVETTES The substantial oysters from the bay of Arcachon are often served with small *crépinettes* (flat sausages) – presumably to make up for the oysters' rather bland flavour.

CÈPE These large, handsome local mushrooms are a great – and costly – delicacy. Fresh or dried, **CÈPES** are much used in sauces with game, particularly **CANARD SAUVAGE** (wild duck). Confusingly, some dishes with

CÈPES are described as **À LA BORDELAISE,** even when no Bordeaux wine is included in the recipe.

ST EMILION AU CHOCOLAT The famous wine town is also known throughout France for its delicious macaroons. This charlotte of chocolate and macaroons is a super-rich pudding in which the almond biscuits are soaked in cognac.

AU COGNAC dishes are most often those in which the spirit is used as a marinade to tenderize as well as flavour meat. An example is the delicately flavoursome **FRICASSÉ DE POULET AU COGNAC,** in which the chicken is marinated for 12 hours, sautéed with small strips of bacon then simmered in the marinade with baby onions. In sauces, cognac is customarily added at a late stage as a flavour enhancer.

LIÈVRE Hare recipes abound. **LIÈVRE EN CHABESSARD** is an elaborate dish in which the hare, stuffed with several meats, garlic and spices and the inevitable shallots, is arranged into a circular shape to fit the special *chabessard* pan in which it is cooked.

CHAUDRÉE Fish chowder is to the Charente what bouillabaisse is to the Côte d'Azur – but made with the plentiful fish of the Atlantic

rather than drawing on the dwindling resources of the Mediterranean. There are numerous versions of *chaudrée,* the most substantial of which provide an entire meal in themselves.

MELON Arguably the best-known product of the Charente besides cognac, the delicious local melons are small and perfectly spherical with green, segmented skin and fragrant, orange flesh. Commonly served in halves with a generous helping of *pineau des charentes,* they are delicious chilled *au naturel* or with a slice of smoked ham such as Bayonne.

MERVEILLES CHARENTAISES The dough for these delicate sweet fritters incorporates a measure of cognac.

BERGERAC

PERIGOURDINE as a suffix to dishes on the menus of the region is a happy reminder that Bergerac lies in the gastronomic paradise that is Périgord. The term may signify the use of the famous Périgord truffle in the recipe. In the absence of an astronomical price, the truffle's place may well have been taken by a humbler local speciality, the walnut.

TERRINE The coarse pâté made with thin strips of meat and flavoured with herbs, spices, cognac and truffles (or alternatively with walnuts or pistachios) is a Périgord speciality – particularly with game.

TERRINE DE GIBIER, game terrine made with either hare, partridge, pheasant, or wild duck, also includes veal, ham, pork and chicken livers.

CANARD ET OIE Ducks and geese are hugely overfed to enlarge their livers for the prized **FOIE GRAS** of Périgord. The flesh of the birds provides other delicious specialities too, such as **MAGRETS**, the breasts, which are cooked like steaks and often served with another local delight, **SAUCE AILLADE** – a rich confection of walnuts and walnut oil, garlic and parsley.

A preserved food to take home with you is **CONFIT DE CANARD**, the cooked meat of duck, conserved in its own fat, and crammed into a glass jar. To prepare, scrape the fat off into a frying pan and use it to fry thick-sliced, par-boiled potatoes until golden and crispy to accompany the meat. Heated through in the oven, the confit emerges as a delectable, slightly salty game dish – with no residual fattiness.

POMMES DE TERRE SARLADAISES Look out for this delicious potato dish on Périgord menus. It is a variation on the technique above, with chopped truffle and parsley added during the cooking, and the pressing of the potatoes together to form a sort of cake.

PRUNEAUX Stuffed with a prune purée, prunes are eaten either as confectionery (they are sold in elegant boxes, and can easily be mistaken for chocolates) or used in cooking as a sweet counterpoint to savoury dishes of hare, pork or veal.

A fishing boat moored in a backwater of the Gironde estuary in the Médoc

Hotels and Restaurants

LE ROUZIC

For a great city at the heart of the world's premier winemaking region, Bordeaux boasts surprisingly few outstanding restaurants. This popular establishment close to the Grand Theatre is among the best. Local specialities include *lamproie bordelaise* and delicious cutlets of Pauillac lamb. Closed Sat lunch and Sun.
34 Cours Chapeau Rouge, 33000 Bordeaux.
Tel (56) 44–39–11.

AUBERGE DE LA COMMANDERIE

Comfortable inn on the St Emilion ramparts, with a simple but delicious menu and fair prices. Restaurant closed Tue from Dec to Feb.
Rue des Cordeliers, St Emilion 33330.
Tel (57) 24–70–19.

HOSTELLERIE PLAISANCE

In the attractive square atop St Emilion, a stylish restaurant, with a few rooms. Closed January.
Place du Clocher, 33330 St Emilion.
Tel (57) 24–72–32.

CITADELLE

Within the splendid citadel of Blaye, with fine views over the Gironde, a comfortable hotel-restaurant with reasonable prices.
33390 Blaye.
Tel (57) 42–17–10.

RELAIS DE MARGAUX

New, expensive hotel with every modern facility, conveniently located in the heart of the Médoc – which is not an area renowned for its comfortable hotels. Closed Dec, Jan and Feb.
33460 Margaux.
Tel (56) 88–38–30.

RESTAURANT DU SQUARE

Simple bistro popular with visitors to the famous Médoc village of St Julien. The *ris de veau* is recommended. Inexpensive.
Place du Monument, 33250 St Julien-Beychevelle.
Tel (56) 59–08–26.

LE LION D'OR

Simple hotel with good, friendly restaurant in the village of St Laurent-Médoc. *Magret grillé sur sarments* (duck breast cooked over vine prunings) is a delicious speciality.
Rue C-Maumey, 33112 St Laurent-Médoc.
Tel (56) 59–40–21.

LA RESERVE

Small and very pleasant hotel in the Graves village of L'Alouette-Pessac (in fact in the suburbs of Bordeaux). Close to Château Haut-Brion – and to the international airport. Comfortable restaurant. Not cheap. Closed mid-Nov to end Feb.
Avenue de Bourgailh, 33600 Pessac.
Tel (56) 07–13–28.

HOSTELLERIE DU CHÂTEAU DE ROLLAND

Excellent restaurant with nine rooms in Barsac. Originally a Carthusian monastery, beautifully converted, it is an ideal base from which to explore the Barsac-Sauternes district. Restaurant closed Wed lunch from Nov to Easter.
Barsac, 33720 Potensac.
Tel (56) 27–15–75.

CLAUDE DARROZE

One of the great restaurants (it also has rooms) of the Bordeaux region, in the southern-Graves town of Langon, near Sauternes. Try the classic *assiette des poissons* – fresh fish in season – with a bottle of dry white Graves. Prices are very fair indeed. Closed 15 Oct–4 Nov and 4–24 Jan.
95 Cours Général-Leclerc, 33210 Langon.
Tel (56) 63–00–48.

L'ETAPE

Comfortable hotel (22 rooms) with simple, good-value restaurant. Open all year. Restaurant closed Sun.
2 Avenue d'Angoulême, 16100 Cognac.
Tel (45) 32–16–15.

MOULIN DE CIERZAC

Highly rated hotel-restaurant 13 kilometres south of Cognac, with picturesque riverside setting.

The arcaded square in the medieval village of Montpazier

Prices are good for the quality of the cooking. Excellent seafood dishes. Closed Feb, and Sun dinner and Mon, Nov–Mar.
Cierzac, 17520 Archiac.
Tel (45) 83–01–32.

LE LOGIS DE BEAULIEU

Just east of the town of Cognac, a pleasant – though not inexpensive – hotel in an attractive parkland setting. The cooking is good and the restaurant is popular with local people. Closed for the Christmas season.
St-Laurent-de-Cognac, 16100 Cognac.
Tel (45) 82–30–50.

RESTAURANT LE CHÂTEAU

Comfortable, good-value restaurant in the heart of the Cognac region's second town, Jarnac. Closed 15 Aug–10 Sept.
Place du Château, 16200 Jarnac.
Tel (45) 81–07–17.

BERGERAC
LE CYRANO

Named, of course, after the famed and entirely fictional character with the elongated nose, this is the top-rated hotel-restaurant in the town of Bergerac. Typical local specialities include roast pigeon and there is a good list of Bergerac wines. Prices are very reasonable. Closed end June to mid-July and Dec, and on Mondays.
2 Boulevard Montaigne, 24100 Bergerac.
Tel (53) 57–02–76.

CENTENAIRE

At Les Eyzies-de-Tayac, a half-hour's drive east of Bergerac, this is a luxury hotel with a famous restaurant (two stars in the *Michelin Guide*). Many Périgord specialities, including *foie gras* and delicious duck and goose dishes. Well worth the detour – and the prices. Closed Nov–Mar. Restaurant closed Tue lunch.
24620 Les Eyzies-de-Tayac.
Tel (53) 06–97–18.

CLOSERIE ST-JACQUES

The best restaurant in Monbazillac, whose menu includes a lavish speciality, lobster cooked in Monbazillac wine. Not cheap. Closed Nov and Jan, and Mon and Tue except in summer.
24240 Monbazillac.
Tel (53) 58–37–77.

AUBERGE DU CHÂTEAU

In Duras, a friendly little hotel with simple rooms and a good restaurant. Reasonable prices. Closed 1–15 Dec and Wed out of season.
47120 Duras.
Tel (53) 83–70–58.

– 91 –

Calendar of Events

JANUARY

18th – Festival of St Vincent in various villages in the Médoc and Graves areas (Gironde)

3rd Sunday – Festival of St Vincent in St Estèphe (Gironde)

APRIL

2nd fortnight – spring wine festival in Gaillac (Tarn)

MAY

Spring wine festival in Bordeaux

Spring wine festival in Fronsac (Gironde)

Spring wine festival in Guyenne (Gironde)

Spring wine festival in Loupiac (Gironde)

Spring wine festival in Pomerol (Gironde)

Spring wine festival in St Emilion (Gironde)

Week of Ascension – Amageais Fair at Eauze (Gers)

21st – Wine festival in Montagne St Emilion (Gironde)

END MAY/BEGINNING JUNE

Wine festival in Pomerol (Gironde)

JUNE

1st weekend – Flower festival in Pauillac (Gironde)

19th – Wine festival at Ste Croix-du-Mont (Gironde)

19th – Flower festival in various villages in the Médoc and Graves areas (Gironde)

3rd week – Flower festival in Loupiac (Gironde)

JULY

14th – Goat cheese fair at Plaisance (Gers)

Weekend nearest 14th – Wine fair in Sigoulès (Dordogne)

End of the month – Beer festival in Thiviers (Dordogne)

AUGUST

Second week – Regional products fair in Riscle (Gers)

Folk dancers at a wine fair in the small village of St Selve

Middle of the month – Wine festival in Gaillac (Tarn)

Middle of the month – Wine and cheese fair in St Aulaye (Dordogne)

SEPTEMBER

First days of the month – Chasselas festival in Moissac (Tarn-et-Garonne)

1st Sunday – Folklore festival of the vines in Burie (Charente-Maritime)

2nd Sunday – Wine-growers' festival in Cazeneuve (Gers)

12th – Wine festival in Bordeaux (Gironde)

12th – Wine festival in Fronsac (Gironde)

18th – Ban des vendanges (announcement of the harvest) in various villages in the Médoc and Graves areas (Gironde)

19th – Announcement of the harvest in St Emilion (Gironde)

Middle of the month – Harvest festival in Amarans (Tarn)

Middle of the month – Harvest festival in Tauriac (Tarn)

4th Sunday – Announcement of the harvest in St Emilion (Gironde)

Last Sunday – Harvest festival in Albas (Lot)

OCTOBER

1st Sunday – Harvest festival in Pouillon (Landes)

1st Sunday – Harvest festival in Semussac (Charente-Maritime)

2nd Sunday – Harvest festival in Berneuil (Charente-Maritime)

2nd Sunday – Harvest festival in Clavette (Charente-Maritime)

2nd Sunday – Wine harvest festival in les Réaux (Charente-Maritime)

2nd Sunday – Harvest festival in Rouffiac (Charente-Maritime)

3rd Sunday – Wine harvest festival in Breuillet (Charente-Maritime)

3rd Sunday – Wine harvest fair in St Porchaire (Charente-Maritime)

Last Sunday – Harvest festival in Cassaigne (Gers)

Last Sunday – Festival of La Gerlande in Fronsac (Gironde)

Last Sunday – Wine harvest ball in Fronton (Haute-Garonne)

Last Sunday – Harvest festival at St Rome-de-Cernon (Aveyron)

30th/31st – Harvest festival in Beauvais-sur-Matha (Charente-Maritime)

NOVEMBER

Harvest festival in Chaniers (Charente-Maritime)

2nd fortnight – New wine festival in Gaillac (Tarn)

20th – Autumn festival in Guyenne (Gironde)

Index